COOKING
WITH
ITALIAN STYLE

GIUNTI

Redazione e impaginazione: Edimedia Sas, Firenze
Fotografie: Arc-en-ciel, Archivio Demetra
Disegni: Mario Steppele

ISBN 88-09-02543-1

Ristampa	Anno
6 5 4 3 2 1	2006 2005 2004 2003 2002

Stampato presso Giunti Industrie Grafiche S.p.A. - Stabilimento di Prato

INTRODUCTION

Italy...

A nation of artists, saints, sailors and... cooks.

The artists, the saints and the sailors have come and gone, but the great Italian food remains.

The preparation of food is a real Italian art today. Recipes with a thousand flavours and colours, the extraordinary results of imagination and creativity, from a generous land.

Italy is made up of sea and sun, of mists and plains, of pure air and high mountains, of the golden ears of corn and sunny hillsides, of... ports and mysterious islands.

Italy is made up of many customs that are exchanged and intertwined with the worlds that have passed through...

Italy is history, the history of the rich, of nobles, of monks and priests, and of great poverty.

All this, garnished with extra virgin olive oil, has brought to life Italian cooking, Mediterranean cooking, the cooking of people who believe in the spiritual values of a good plate of pasta with beans.

HORS D'OEUVRES

MARINATED ANCHOVIES

◀ *Campania* ▶

500 g of fresh anchovies, 1 lemon, 2-3 bay leaves, 1 sprig of parsley, 1 l of white wine vinegar, extra virgin olive oil, salt.

Clean the anchovies, discarding the heads and the backbone (it should be possible to remove both with a single swift movement), wash and dry them. Place them in a deep-sided glass or ceramic bowl together with the bay leaves, the grated lemon rind (only the outer yellow part) and the parsley. Cover with the vinegar, which has previously been boiled, and leave to marinate. After approx. 4 hours, drain the anchovies and place them in another deep ceramic dish, add salt and just cover with oil.

ITALIAN HORS D'OEUVRE

◆

This is the simple hors d'oeuvre of sliced meats, the success of which depends above all on the care taken over the way in which it is brought to the table and on a suitable accompaniment of different kinds of bread, bread sticks, pickles and preserves in oil, butter curls, anchovies, grilled and raw vegetables (without disdaining to add fruit like melons, figs, pears, etc. suitable for serving together with savoury foods).

Generally raw ham is placed with one end of each slice inside a bowl placed in the centre of the serving plate, so that it drapes outside forming a kind of cascade, the slices slightly overlaying each other. An attractive new idea is to create a bowl from a melon; cut off the upper part and, with a special instrument, remove the pulp and from this make lots of small balls to be presented on the table in a glass bowl with ice. Cooked ham and slices of coarse-grained salami can be folded in two and placed on a serving plate side by side.

Roll up the slices of fine-grained salamis and Bologna sausage to create cones; these can be dressed with sliced pickled cucumbers placed in a fan shape or with Parmesan cheese cut into thin sticks.

The presentation of the pickles must also be prepared carefully: they can be placed in small wooden bowls or on a single serving place on which lettuce leaves have been put to serve as bowls.

On the table baskets should be placed here and there with bread, bread sticks, toasted garlic bread, toasted rolls and a few bowls containing butter curls.

AUBERGINE HORS D'OEUVRE
◀ *Calabria* ▶

4 aubergines, 4 cloves of garlic, 1 sprig of basil, 2 spoonfuls of apple vinegar, ¹/₂ glass of extra virgin olive oil, salt, home-made type bread.

Wash the aubergines, slice them longwise and leave them to release their liquid by covering them with a little salt. In the meantime, finely chop the basil and add it to the crushed garlic, mix with the oil, the vinegar and the salt to form a sauce.

Rinse the salt from the aubergines and grill them on both sides for a few minutes. Take them from the grill and put them into a salad bowl, pour over the basil and garlic sauce and toss them, then leave them to stand in a cool place for at least 10 hours. Serve together with lightly toasted slices of bread.

PARMESAN AND TRUFFLE HORS D'OEUVRES
◆

250 g of Parmesan cheese, 2 medium sized white truffles, ¹/₂ lemon, butter, 2 spoonfuls of extra virgin olive oil, salt and pepper.

Accurately clean the truffles using a small brush and a clean cloth. Slice them with a truffle slicer and lay half of the slices on the bottom of a buttered oven dish. Sprinkle lightly with a little salt and pepper, then cover the slices with half of the Parmesan cheese cut into paper thin slices. Pour a little oil over.

Make a second layer the same as the first. Put the oven dish into a preheated oven for approximately ten minutes. After removing from the oven, sprinkle with the juice of the squeezed lemon.

9

Bagna caûda
◀ *The Aosta Valley, Piedmont* ▶

200 g of salted anchovies, 200 g of garlic, 250 dl of extra virgin olive oil, 40 g of butter.

Carefully remove the salt from the salted anchovies with a clean cloth and remove the backbones; cut the anchovies into small pieces and place them in an earthenware bowl together with the very finely sliced garlic. Cover with oil and cook on a low heat, placing a wire net under the bowl to protect it from the flames.
The heat must be very gentle in order not to brown the garlic. Stir occasionally, taking care that the anchovies do not break up.
After approximately 30 minutes, melt the butter in the bowl and bring to the table on a special *bagna caûda* stove to keep the sauce hot.
Raw vegetables (cardoons, sweet peppers, celery, endive, radishes, etc.) and cooked (onions, beetroot, roasted sweet peppers, etc.) are cut into pieces and immersed in the *bagna caûda*.
For a lighter version, leave the garlic to stand in milk for a few hours before slicing it, then to flavour the oil place the garlic in the oil and begin to heat; remove it from the heat before adding the anchovies. In this case, a white truffle sliced extremely thinly can be added to the sauce before serving.

10

Shrimp boats
◆ 📷

For the putt-pastry: 125 g of flour, 125 g of butter, 1 egg, salt.

For the filling: 50 g of shrimps, 50 g bolete of mushrooms, 2 spoonfuls of onion grass, 1 spoonful of sherry, lemon juice, 20 g of salted butter, $1/2$ spoonful of sour cream, salt, pepper.

To prepare the pastry, use chilled tools and ice cold water. Mix the flour and a pinch of salt with a glass of ice cold water until you have a thick smooth dough, cover with a cloth and leave to stand in a cool, dark place. With wet fingers, work the butter until it is the same consistency as the dough, then make it into a rectangular shape.

Roll out the dough on a well floured work surface, then place the butter in the centre; fold the layer of dough in two, with the butter in between and press lightly with the rolling pin to amalgamate the butter into the dough, leave to stand for 5 minutes.

Then begin working the flaky pastry, carrying out the "folding" which is necessary to produce fragrant and crumbly pastry. Keep the flour at hand to keep the work surface and the rolling pin well floured.

Roll out the pastry, always keeping it to a rectangular shape one centimetre thick, fold it in three and roll it out again, fold again in three in the other direction and roll out again. Leave it to stand in the refrigerator for approx. 15 minutes.

Repeat the same procedures including leaving it to stand in the refrigerator twice more (it must be folded six times in all), then the pastry is ready. Roll out the pastry and cut out little "boats" with an oval cutter, cook in the oven at 180°C for about ten minutes. Wash the shrimps and place them in a dish with bowling water for about ten minutes, then shell them and delicately dry them. Melt the salted butter in an earthenware casserole, add the mushrooms and fry lightly for a minute.

Pour over the sour cream to which has been added a little lemon juice and bring to the boil, stirring with a wooden spoon.

Fold in the shrimps and the lemon grass, add salt and pepper to taste, and flavour with the sherry. Take off the heat and leave to cool.

Fill the "boats" with this sauce and serve.

SAGE BISCUITS
◀ _Basilicata_ ▶

500 g of flour, 1 packet of baking powder for savoury cakes, 1 glass of milk, 1 sprig of sage, 150 g of butter, 1 spoonful of salt.

Put the flour and the baking powder in a large bowl with the salt, the finely chopped sage leaves and the melted butter. Gradually add the milk. Stir the mixture well.

Roll out the pastry to a thickness of approx. 1 cm and with a round cutter (or with the top of a glass) cut out round biscuits. Place them on a buttered baking pan. Cook in a pre-heated oven for about ten minutes.

BRUSCHETTA
(OLIVE OIL TOAST)
◀ *Lazio* ▶

Home-made type bread, garlic, extra virgin olive oil, salt.

Bruschetta is widespread and found in almost all the southern regions of Italy, all of which claim to have invented this tasty hors d'oeuvres. Cut the bread into slices about 1 cm thick and toast them (preferably on a wood fire). Just before serving, rub one side with a clove of garlic, sprinkle it with a little salt and dribble over it a very good olive oil. Serve hot.
The version with tomatoes is excellent: a layer of tomato sauce is spread on the slices of bread and then flavoured with basil, salt, pepper and oil. Instead of the sauce fresh tomatoes can be used which – after removing the seeds and the excess liquid – are cut into small cubes. Rub the surface of the toasted bread with the garlic, then place the tomato cubes on the bread, and dress with a little extra virgin olive oil.

SCALLOPS AU GRATIN
◀ *Veneto* ▶

2-3 scallops per person, breadcrumbs, 1 sprig of parsley, cognac, butter, salt, pepper in grains.

Clean the scallops, eliminating the flat part of the shell and separating the molluscs from their shells. Mix together a few spoonfuls of bread-crumbs with the finely chopped parsley, a pinch of salt, a little freshly ground pepper and a drop of cognac (the mixture must not be too damp). Cover the molluscs with bread-crumbs, then replace them in their shells again, pour over a drop of cognac and place a knob of butter on each one.
Leave the bread-crumbed scallops to brown in a hot oven for about ten minutes. Serve piping hot.

CAZZILLI
◀ *Sicily* ▶

1 kg of potatoes, 1 clove of garlic, 1 sprig of parsley, 2 eggs, breadcrumbs, olive oil, salt, pepper.

Boil the potatoes, peel them, and mash them with a potato masher; amalgamate the crushed garlic and the finely chopped parsley to the potato purée, add salt and pepper to taste.
Leave to cool a little, then form oval balls. Roll them in the beaten egg, then cover with breadcrumbs. Fry in hot oil. Drain on absorbent paper, sprinkle with salt and serve the *cazzilli* hot.

SHRIMP COCKTAIL
◆

For the Aurora sauce: mayonnaise, 2 spoonfuls of tomato ketchup, 2 spoonfuls of single cream, 1 spoonful of cognac.
For the filling: 500 g of shelled shrimps, 1 let-

tuce heart, 1 sprig of dill, Tabasco sauce, salt, white pepper, croutons.

Amalgamate the mayonnaise with the tomato ketchup, the cream and a drop of Tabasco sauce. Add the shrimps. Place the washed lettuce leaves into individual bowls and place a few spoonfuls of shrimps covered in sauce on top. Serve the cocktail chilled and decorated with the dill, and accompany with the croutons.

STUFFED MUSSELS
◀ *The Marches* ▶

1 kg of mussels, 300 g of firm, ripe tomatoes, 1 sprig of parsley, 1 clove of garlic, breadcrumbs, extra virgin olive oil, salt, pepper.

Scrape the mussels (or muscles as they are called in the Marches region) under running water and open them in a pan over a hot flame. As they open, discard the empty half of the shell and place the other half, containing the mussel, on an oven tray.
Place the tomatoes in boiling water for a moment, remove them from the water and peel them, remove the seeds and chop finely. Mix the tomatoes with the crushed garlic and the finely chopped parsley, add salt and freshly ground pepper, oil and a few spoonfuls of breadcrumbs, to form a firm, consistent but soft mixture. Spread this dressing on the mussels and pour a little more oil over them. Leave to brown in a pre-heated oven for about ten minutes. For an alternative version of this recipe, add a little roughly minced raw ham (approx. 50 g) to the mixture for the filling.

CHICKEN LIVER CROUTONS
◀ *Umbria* ▶

Slices of home-made type bread, 250 g of chicken livers, 1 spring onion, 3 anchovies, 1 spoonful of capers, white wine, butter, salt, pepper in grains.

Lightly fry the spring onion with a knob of butter; add the chicken livers, add a little white wine and salt; when the liquid has evaporated, take off from the heat and mince the contents of the frying pan with the anchovies and the capers. Put back on the heat for a few minutes with a little butter, together with some freshly ground pepper. Spread the mixture on slices of toasted bread.

TRUFFLE CROUTONS
◀ *Umbria* ▶

Slices of bread, black truffle (as much as you wish), anchovy fillets, 1 lemon, extra virgin olive oil.

Carefully clean and wash the truffle, then grate as much as desired for flavouring (this depends mainly on the quality of the truffle). Heat a little oil in a pan and add the

grated truffle, leaving it on the heat for a few moments. Add the minced anchovy fillets and the lemon juice, mixing carefully. Toast the slices of bread, spread the mixture on the slices and serve.

CROUTONS *ALLA CIOCIARA*
◀ *Lazio* ▶

Home-made type bread, fresh goat's milk cheese, firm, ripe tomatoes, stoned black olives, vinegar, extra virgin olive oil, paprika.

Put the cheese, cut into small pieces, the oil and the vinegar into a small pan and place on a low heat; cook gently, stirring to allow the cheese to melt. Just before removing from the heat, add the tomatoes, cut into small cubes, the stoned olives cut into small pieces, and a pinch of paprika. Leave for a moment for the mixture to absorb the flavours while you toast the slices of bread. Arrange the slices of toasted bread on a plate and place the sauce on each slice.

ERBAZZONE
(TASTY SPINACH PIE)
◀ *Emilia Romagna* ▶

1 kg of spinach, 100 g of wheat flour, 60 g of lard, 100 g of un-smoked bacon, 1 small onion, 1 clove of garlic, 300 g of bread crumbs, 200 g of Parmesan cheese, 4 eggs, salt, pepper.

Carefully clean and wash the spinach and cook it in boiling water, squeeze out the water and mince it finely. While the spinach is boiling, prepare a dough with the flour, the lard, water and salt. Make this into a ball and leave to stand for about half an hour in the refrigerator.

Peel the onion and the garlic, mince them together with the bacon and fry lightly. Add the spinach. Apart, mix together the breadcrumbs, the grated Parmesan cheese, the eggs and a little salt.

Remove the dough ball from the refrigerator. Divide it into two parts and roll out two pastry circles about 1 cm thick. Butter a pie tin and place in it one of the pastry circles to make the base of the pie; fill the pie with the spinach mixture, then cover with the other pastry circle. Prick the surface with the prongs of a fork, and cook in a warm oven (about 160°C) for about half an hour. Remove from the oven and serve sliced, hot or cold.

FETTUNTA
(OILED SLICES)
◀ *Tuscany* ▶

4 slices of slightly stale home-made type bread, 2 cloves of garlic, extra virgin olive oil, salt, pepper in grains.

This is extremely simple to prepare, and its success depends above all on the quality of the olive oil (cold pressed oil is best).
Slightly toast the slices of bread, cut from loaves at least a day old, on an open fire (or under the grill). As soon as they are crusty, rub the surface with a garlic clove and sprinkle on it a pinch of salt and a generous dose of freshly ground black pepper. Pour on a trickle of oil and serve immediately, while still very hot and before the oil

has completely sunk into the bread. During the winter, *fettunta* can be prepared with black cabbage, previously boiled in salted water and well drained, placed on top.

LEMON CRABS
◀ *Veneto* ▶

1 medium sized crab per person, 1 lemon, parsley, extra virgin olive oil, salt, pepper.

Boil the crabs in plenty of salted water (possibly flavoured with onion, bay leaves and parsley). After 30 minutes, remove and drain, and leave to cool. Remove the back part of the legs, keeping aside the coral. Take the pulp from both the body and the legs of the crabs and clean the shells thoroughly. Replace the pulp into the shells and pour over a trickle of oil, a little lemon juice, salt and pepper. Serve garnished with the coral and the finely chopped parsley.

15

SEA FOOD SALAD
◀ *Campania* ▶

3 kg of shell fish of various kinds (mussels, cockles, razor clams, etc.), 6 cuttlefish, 1-2 lemons, 3 cloves of garlic, 1 sprig of parsley, 1 bay leaf, salt, pepper in grains.

Clean the cuttlefish; if they are very small, leave them whole, otherwise separate the tentacles from the heads and cut each head into 3-4 pieces. Toss them into salted boiling water, together with the a few slices of lemon, the bay leaf and a few grains of pepper; boil for 3-4 minutes, then drain well.

Clean the molluscs thoroughly and remove any intestines, then put them into a frying pan with a few spoonfuls of oil and crushed garlic. Open the shells of the shellfish by turning up the heat; remove the shells and filter off and put aside the liquid remaining in the pan.

Place the shelled molluscs, the shellfish and the cuttlefish all together in a serving bowl. Add lemon juice, pepper and finely chopped parsley to the filtered liquid that was put aside, and pour over the fish. The salad will be tastier if served warm.

RUSSIAN SALAD

◆

200 g of small peas, 150 g of green beans, 2 potatoes, 2 carrots, 1 small turnip, 100 g of mixed pickles, 100 g of pickled onions, 2 spoonfuls of capers, stoned green olives, 2 eggs, 2 cups of mayonnaise, olive oil, salt.

Wash and clean the vegetables, shell the peas, cut the tops and tails off the green beans and cut into small pieces about 1 cm long, peel the turnip, the potatoes and the carrots and cut them into cubes. Boil the vegetables separately in boiling salted water (place only the potatoes in cold water and then bring to the boil), removing them from the water and draining them when they are still a little crisp. Mix the vegetables together in a large bowl together with the mixed pickles (cut any large ones into small cubes), the pickled onions and the capers; dress with oil.

Mix the vegetables into half of the mayonnaise. Spread the rest of the mayonnaise on top of the vegetable mixture and garnish as desired with slices of hard-boiled eggs and olives.

SWEET PEPPER ROULADES

◆

2 sweet peppers (1 yellow and 1 red), 50 g of fresh goat's milk cheese, 50 g of mild Gorgonzola, parsley, paprika.

Wash the peppers and scorch them on the gas flame or under the grill; leave them to cool, then remove the white inner skin and the seeds, and cut into rather wide slices. In a bowl amalgamate the goat's milk cheese with the Gorgonzola, and add a pinch of pepper and a spoonful of washed and finely chopped fresh parsley to flavour.

Spread the mixture onto the pepper slices, roll up the slices, fix them with toothpicks and keep them in a cool place until serving.

MOZZARELLA *IN CARROZZA*
◀ *Campania* ▶ 📷

8 slices of slightly stale bread, 1 large mozzarella, 2 eggs, anchovies in oil (optional), white flour, milk, olive oil, salt, pepper.

Cut the mozzarella into rather thick slices and place each one between two slices of bread; if desired, these can be flavoured adding a carefully cleaned and de-salted, boned anchovy filet. Press each "sandwich" and cover first with flour, then with beaten egg to which has been added the milk, salt and pepper. When the bread is saturated, drain and brown on each side in abundant hot oil.

Remove the "mozzarellas in carriages" from the pan and drain on absorbent paper; serve hot.

CALF'S HEAD* IN SALAD
◀ *Lombardy* ▶

600 g of calf's head, 2 onions, 1 clove of garlic, 2 spoonfuls of finely chopped parsley, 1 teaspoonful of finely chopped thyme, 3 spoonfuls of vinegar, 1 dl of extra virgin olive oil, paprika, salt.

Put a saucepan on the heat with plenty of water flavoured with the thyme. When it begins to boil, add salt and place the calf's head into the water; cook for 2 hours. Remove the head from the liquid and leave to cool. In the meanwhile, clean and cut the onions and garlic into very thin slices, and prepare a mixture of oil, vinegar, salt and a pinch of pepper in a bowl. Cut the head into small pieces and place in the oil-vinegar mixture, stirring well, then add the finely sliced onion and garlic. Sprinkle with the chopped parsley and serve.

This is an excellent hors d'oeuvres, which can be served warm or cold, but it is also a tasty main course for a summer lunch. If served cold, do not place in the refrigerator, because this will cause the meat to become tough.

*Calf's head is not the whole head of the calf, but rather the brains.

ASCOLIAN OLIVES
◀ *The Marches* ▶

1 kg of green Ascolian olives (from the Ascoli area), 150 g of veal, 150 g of minced pork, 100 g of raw ham, 100 g of grated sheep's milk cheese and Parmesan cheese, 2 spoonfuls of tomato pulp, 4 eggs, nutmeg, bread crumbs, white flour, white wine, extra virgin olive oil, salt, pepper.

Lightly fry the meat in a frying pan with a little oil; add salt and pepper and the wine; when the wine has evaporated cover the pan and finish cooking. In a bowl, mix the cooked meat with the minced ham, the cheese and a small quantity of bread crumbs, a pinch of nutmeg, the tomato pulp and 2 of the eggs; amalgamate the mixture well to obtain a soft, firm paste.
Remove the stones from the olives with a special tool and fill them with the paste. Roll the stuffed olives in the flour, put them in the 2 beaten eggs and then cover them with breadcrumbs. Fry them in hot oil and serve piping hot.

GARNISHED OLIVES
◀ *Puglia* ▶

Giant black olives, fresh hot red peppers, dried hot red peppers, parsley, extra virgin olive oil.

Drain the olives and lightly score them, then place them in the marinade of oil with the minced fresh

peppers, the finely chopped dried red peppers and the crushed garlic. Leave to marinate for 24 hours in a covered bowl, shaking it every now and then.

After marinating for this period, the olives can be served at any time (within a few days), sprinkled with finely chopped parsley.

FRIED OLIVES
◀ *Sicily* ▶

40 large black olives, 2 cloves of garlic, marjoram, 1 small glass vinegar, extra virgin olive oil.

Heat the oil in a pan, place the crushed garlic cloves in the hot oil and lightly fry for a few minutes. Add the olives and the vinegar; reduce the liquid and flavour with the marjoram. Serve piping hot.

PANZEROTTI (TOMATO "TUMMIES")
◀ *Puglia* ▶

<u>For the pasta</u>: *400 g of white flour, 25 g of fresh yeast, 50 g of extra virgin olive oil, salt.*
<u>For the filling</u>: *250 g of mozzarella cheese, 400 g of small ripe tomatoes, marjoram, extra virgin olive oil, salt, paprika.*

First arrange the flour into a mound on the pastry board. Make a well in the centre and crumble the yeast into it, dissolve it with a spoonful of warm water, add salt, oil and enough water to obtain a dough that can be easily worked. Knead the dough energetically, until it is soft and elastic: it has to have a consistency similar to that of an earlobe. Make the dough into a ball,

cover with flour, then cover with a damp cloth and leave it to rise in a warm place protected from draughts for about 2½ hours.

In the meanwhile prepare the filling: peel the tomatoes (after placing them for a moment in boiling water to facilitate this operation), remove the seeds, and heat the tomatoes in a pan with a little extra virgin olive oil until the liquid has evaporated; add marjoram, the paprika and salt, then switch off the heat. Take the dough and knead it for a few minutes, then divide it into 8-10 parts; roll out each part, making a thin circle. In the centre of each circle place the mozzarella cut into small cubes with a little of the tomato sauce, flavouring with a little more pepper and marjoram if desired, fold the circles in half and close them to make half moon shapes, dampen the edges and press them together to close them.

Fry them in hot oil, turning them to brown them uniformly; remove and drain them on absorbent paper. Serve piping hot.

SAGE IN BATTER

200 g of large sage leaves, 100 g of flour, 2 eggs, ½ lemon, olive oil, salt.

Clean, wash and dry the sage leaves. In a bowl, mix the flour, the lemon juice, a spoonful of oil, one of water and the stiffly whisked whites of the eggs. Immerge the sage leaves into this batter and fry them in hot oil, serving them warm, if possible. Alternatively, the eggs can be substituted by a few spoonfuls of milk.

PILCHARDS *IN SAÓR*
◀ *Veneto* ▶ 📷

700 g of fresh pilchards, 700 g of onions, 1 lemon, 1 handful of raisins, 3 bay leaves, 3 cloves, white flour, 2 glassfuls of vinegar, olive oil, salt, pepper.

Soften the raisins in warm water. Clean the pilchards, removing the heads and bones; wash them and leave them to dry on a clean cloth. Cover them with flour and fry them in hot water; drain them on absorbent paper.
In the oil used for cooking the pilchards, lightly fry the onions cut into thin rings, add two glassfuls of vinegar and the grated lemon rind. Cook for a couple of minutes.
In a glass jar place a layer of the fried fish, sprinkle with a little salt and pepper and cover with a layer of onions adding the cloves and the raisins; continue placing layer on layer, alternating the ingredients, until the onions are finished. Cover and keep in the refrigerator for a few days before tasting.
Apart from the raisins, pine kernels or apple slices can also be added. The *saór*, or flavour – one of the tastiest methods of conservation typical of the Veneto region – is suitable for most kinds of fish, from the miniscule fish, usually simply fried, to the larger kinds, like sole.

MOZZARELLA TITBITS
◀ *Puglia* ▶

100 g of small mozzarella balls, green olives, marjoram, extra virgin olive oil.

Cut the mozzarella balls, preferably of buffalo milk, into halves or quarters; brush them with a little oil and sprinkle them with fresh marjoram. Stone the olives, then spear the mozzarella pieces and the olives with tooth picks, one piece of mozzarella and one olive on each toothpick.
Alternatively, the marjoram can be substituted by sweet paprika, or with finely chopped basil.

EASTER CAKE
◀ *Liguria* ▶ 📷

For the dough: 600 g of flour, 2 spoonfuls of extra virgin olive oil, salt.
For the filling: 8 artichokes, 400 g of ricotta cheese, 100 g of butter, 10 eggs, 50 g of grated Parmesan cheese, 1 clove of garlic, parsley, marjoram, 1 lemon, 2 spoonfuls of flour, salt.

Remove the hard outer leaves, the stem and the sharp points from the artichokes; cut them lengthwise into thin slices and leave them in water with the juice of the lemon.
Sift the flour and make it into a mound on the work surface, make a well in the centre and pour in the oil, $\frac{1}{2}$ litre of warm water, and the salt; knead the dough for 15 minutes, until it is soft. Cover with a damp cloth, then with a dry one on top, and leave to stand.
Wash the leaves of the herbs, boil them in a little salted water, drain well and squeeze to remove the excess liquid. Melt 50 g of butter in the frying pan and lightly fry the garlic, then add the well-drained artichokes, cover and leave to cook gently. When cooked, add a little finely chopped parsley.

Remove the artichokes from the pan, add the herbs to the liquid remaining in the pan. Leave to cool, then remove the garlic.

Put into a bowl the ricotta, the grated Parmesan, 3 eggs, the flour, salt and pepper and mix well. Add the cooled herb mixture and artichokes. Take the dough and divide it into ten pieces, always keeping the parts not being worked under a cloth to prevent them becoming dry. With a rolling pin roll out four of the pieces of dough (one at a time) very thinly.

Lay the pastry layers one on the other in a baking tray, brushing the first three with oil; press the bottom layer well down on the bottom of the dish, and stick the layers together at the edges, allowing them to protrude for about 1 cm.

Pour the prepared filling onto the top layer; with the back of a spoon make seven cavities in the filling and into each one break an egg and a spoonful of melted butter, a spoonful of Parmesan, salt and pepper.

Now place the other layers of dough on top, proceeding as before, brushing each one with a little oil. Cut off the excess dough from the sides, and with these pieces form a plait to place around the top edge.

Brush the top layer of dough with oil and prick it with a fork, being careful not to break the eggs. Cook the cake in a moderate oven for about an hour, until the top is golden brown.

Serve hot.

SQUID SALAD
◀ *Tuscany* ▶

500 g of very fresh squid, 1 sprig of radishes, 2 carrots, 3 sticks of white celery, 1 stick of green celery, ¹/₂ fennel, ¹/₂ onion, 1 leek, 1 bay leaf, extra virgin olive oil, salt, pepper in grains.

Wash the squid and boil them in slightly salted water flavoured with the green celery, the onion and the bay leaf. When they are cooked, drain them and cut them into thin strips; put the strips into a large bowl.

Clean and wash all the vegetables, slice the white celery, the fen-

nel, the carrots and the white parts of the leek, leaving the radishes whole. Delicately mix the vegetables and the squid together, add salt, freshly ground pepper and abundant extra virgin olive oil.

SHRIMP VOL-AU-VENTS
◆

12 vol-au-vent cases, 300 g of shelled shrimps, 100 g of button mushroom heads, 1 small leek, parsley, 2 dl of milk, 2 spoonfuls of flour, 25 g of butter, salt, pepper.

Mince or grate the leek and fry in the butter for 5 minutes; stir in the flour and add the milk gradually.

Cook for a few more minutes, add salt and pepper. Add the sliced mushrooms to this sauce, then the shelled shrimps (put aside a few whole shrimps for garnishing) and cook, stirring continuously, for 4-5 minutes.

Place the filling into the vol-au-vent cases and put into a pre-heated oven at 200°C for a few minutes, then serve garnished with the whole shrimps and sprinkled with finely chopped parsley.

MUSHROOM VOL-AU-VENTS

◀ *The Aosta Valley, Piedmont* ▶ 📷

4 vol-au-vent cases, 10 button mushrooms, 50 g of Taleggio cheese, 20 g of butter, paprika, salt, pepper.

◆ Lightly fry the sliced mushrooms in butter for about 10 minutes, with a little salt and pepper.

◆ Put the cheese in a bowl and work in freshly ground black pepper, salt, a pinch of paprika and the liquid remaining from the cooking of the mushrooms.

◆ Fill the vol-au-vents with the cheese paste, garnish with mushrooms and put into a pre-heated oven just long enough to warm through.

LEAVENED BREADS, FLAT BREADS, PIZZAS, SAVOURY CAKES

FARINATA
(CHICK PEA BREAD)
◀ *Liguria* ▶

350 g of chickpea flour, rosemary, extra virgin olive oil, salt.

In a bowl mix the chickpea flour with a litre of water and leave to stand overnight. The next day, remove any froth which may have formed on the surface, and add to the mixture half a glassful of oil and a little salt.
Pour into a baking tray greased with oil and put into a moderate oven until it is well cooked. Take out of the oven, sprinkle with rosemary and serve piping hot.

FLAT OLIVE
OIL BREAD
◀ *Liguria* ▶

500 g of flour, 30 g of yeast, 1 dl of extra virgin olive oil, salt.

Dissolve the yeast in a cup of tepid water, add it to the flour and knead well to obtain a soft dough; cover with a cloth and leave to stand for about 2 hours in a warm place. When the dough has risen, roll it out on a baking tray (greased with oil and sprinkled with salt) making sure that it is no more than 2 cm thick. Pinch the surface with your fingers, sprinkle with salt and oil, put into a hot oven for about 20 minutes. Serve hot (although it is also excellent cold).

Among the many alternatives to this basic recipe we suggest this simple variation: before putting it into the oven, sprinkle the surface with rosemary.

FLAT CHEESY BREAD
◀ *Liguria* ▶

For the dough: 350 g of flour, 15 g of fresh yeast, 1 spoonful of extra virgin olive oil, salt, 400 g of soft cheese (e.g. Fontina), extra virgin olive oil.

Dissolve the yeast in a little warm water, then make a mound of the flour on the pastry board, together with the oil and salt. Knead the dough adding warm water, until it is soft and elastic, then make it into a ball and leave it for a couple of hours to rise in a warm place protected from draughts and covered with a damp cloth. When it has doubled in size, divide the dough into two parts,

knead it a little more, then roll it out on a pastry board, forming two thickish rounds. Grease the baking tray, place one of the rounds on it, cover with the cheese cut into thin slices; place the second round on top, and sticking them together round the edges.

Dribble a little oil over and prick the surface lightly with a fork and cook in the oven at 250°C for about 20 minutes.

WALNUT BREAD

◆

300 g of flour, 400 g of walnut kernels, 300 g of honey, 4 eggs, 1 lemon, 600 g of milk, 25 g of fresh or dried yeast, olive oil, salt

Mix the ingredients together to form a smooth dough. Divide the dough into a number of small rolls. Grease the oven tray with oil and flour it, place the rolls on it and leave to stand for about half an hour, for them to rise. Cook in a pre-heated hot oven (200 °C) for approx. 40 minutes.

CARASAU BREAD OR CARTA MUSICA

◄ *Sardinia* ►

1 kg of durum wheat flour, 10 g of yeast, 1 spoonfuls of coarse salt.

Dissolve the yeast in a little warm water, and the salt in no more than 5 dl of warm water.

Mix the yeast with the flour and knead it together with the salted water, until it is soft and damp, but well amalgamated. Form dough balls about 8 cm in diameter and leave them to rise for about 4 hours in a dry place. Roll out the balls with a rolling pin, keeping them constantly floured in order not to stick to the rolling pin or the pastry board, and form rounds about 2-3 mm thick and about 40 cm in diameter. Cook the pastry rounds in a hot oven and, when they have risen, separate the upper surface from the lower. At this point, this kind of bread in Sardinia is called *lentu* and it is soft and fragrant.

To obtain more crispy bread, like the typical *carasau* put them back in the oven and continue cooking until they are dry and crisp.

APULIAN BREAD
◀ *Puglia* ▶

2 kg of flour, 40 g of fresh or dried yeast, 10 g of malt, 40 g of salt.

Dissolve the yeast in a little warm water; then mix all the ingredients together with 1½ litres of water. Knead for about 20 minutes, till the dough is soft and smooth. Cover it and leave it to rise in a sheltered place for about two hours. Knead it again gently and divide it into large rolls; place them in such a way that the dough can only rise vertically, and leave to stand again for half an hour. Then press down on them, turn them upside down

and leave them for another half hour. With the point of a knife, make a circular incision on the surface then place in a hot oven (220°C) for about 40 minutes.

TUSCAN BREAD
◀ *Tuscany* ▶

1.4 kg of soft wheat flour, 60 g of natural yeast.

The typical Tuscan bread is made without salt and is known as *sciocco* (lit. foolish – according to an Italian saying, a stupid person is said to have no *sale in zucca*, that is salt in his pumpkin, no brains in his head), a name that extends into Umbria, and the northern part of Lazio, corresponding to the area occupied by the ancient Etruscan people. The flour is mixed with the yeast and enough warm water to obtain the correct consistency. Knead the dough at length, then leave it to rise for several hours.

When it has risen, divide it into loaves, either long, like French bread, or rolls of various sizes, from 500 g to a kilo or more. Make diagonal cuts across the top surface, then cook in a moderate oven (approx. 210-220°C).

When it is cooked the bread has a holey texture inside and a crusty outer surface. It is eaten in slices and it is the best bread for preparing *bruschetta* croutons and *fettunte*.

ROMAGNA *PIADINA*
◀ *Emilia Romagna* ▶

500 g of flour, 150 g of lard, 1 spoonful of salt.

Mix the flour, the salt and the lard, adding enough water to make a rather stiff dough. Knead the dough for about 10 minutes, divide it into pieces as big as an egg. Roll them out to make thin discs.

As the discs are ready, lay them one on another, flouring them and protecting them with a cloth. Heat an iron pan (a fireproof stone is even better) and cook the *piadine* on both sides, pricking them with a fork. As soon as each pair is cooked, sandwich the filling between them and cover them with a cloth to keep them warm.

They can be eaten with raw ham or cheese, or they can be served as a side dish.

SEA FRUIT PIZZA

◆

For the dough: 400 g of wheat flour, 25 g of fresh yeast, 50 g of extra virgin olive oil, salt.
For the topping: 300 g of shelled shrimps, 100 g of cockles, 100 g of mussels, 700 g of skinned tomatoes, 5 cloves of garlic, 1 sprig of parsley, extra virgin olive oil, salt.

Make a mound of the flour on a large pastry board or a suitable work surface. Make a well in the centre and crumble the yeast into it, dissolve the yeast with a spoonful of warm water, add the salt, oil and as much water as necessary to make a smooth, soft and easily kneaded dough. Knead the dough energetically until it is soft and elastic. Then make the dough into a ball, flour it, cover it with a damp cloth and leave to rise in a warm place sheltered from draughts, for about 2 and a half hours. In the meantime, clean the various kinds of fish. Put the cockles and the mussels in two separate frying pans, each with two cloves of garlic cut into slices and a little oil; mix with a wooden spoon, cover and leave to open spontaneously; remove from the shells (keeping a few for garnishing) and put aside. Scald the shrimps.

Cut the squids into strips and boil them. Beat the skinned tomatoes and flavour them with crushed garlic and finely chopped parsley. Roll out the pizza dough and place on a low-sided oiled oven tray, and place the beaten tomatoes on top. Leave to stand in a warm place for 20 minutes.

Then cook in the oven for 15 minutes, remove from the oven and place the shellfish and the molluscs on the surface. Sprinkle a pinch of salt, the parsley and garlic over it, dribble a little oil over it and put it back in the oven for 10 more minutes, keeping the temperature around 250°C.

Remove from the oven, garnish with the shells kept aside, and serve.

PIZZA MARGHERITA (MARGARET'S PIZZA)

◆

For the dough: 400 g of wheat flour, 25 g of fresh yeast, 50 g of extra virgin olive oil, salt.
For the topping: 400 g of skinned tomatoes, 300 g of fresh mozzarella cheese, basil, marjoram, paprika, extra virgin olive oil, salt.

Make the flour into a mound on a large pastry board or on a suitable work surface. Make a well in the centre and crumble the yeast into it, dissolve the yeast with a spoonful of warm water, add salt, oil and enough water to make a soft, smooth, easily kneaded dough. Knead the dough energetically until it

is soft and elastic, cover it with a damp cloth and leave to rise in a warm place sheltered from draughts for about 2 and a half hours.

Roll out the dough to about half a centimetre thick and place it on an oiled oven tray. Drain the tomatoes and squash them with a fork and place them on the dough, sprinkle a pinch of salt over it and leave it to stand in a warm place for about 20 minutes. Cook it in a hot oven for another 20 minutes, remove it from the oven, place the mozzarella cheese cut into slices on top.

Add the marjoram and the basil to the oil and dribble the oil over it, then put it back into the oven for about ten more minutes before serving.

NEAPOLITAN PIZZA
◀ _Campania_ ▶

For the dough: 400 g of wheat flour, 25 g of fresh yeast, 50 g of extra virgin olive oil, salt.
For the topping: 400 g of skinned tomatoes, 3 cloves of garlic, a few leaves of basil or marjoram, extra virgin olive oil, salt.

Make the flour into a mound on a large pastry board or on a suitable work surface. Make a well in the centre and crumble the yeast into it, dissolve the yeast with a spoonful of warm water, add salt, oil and enough water to make a soft, smooth, easily kneaded dough.

Knead the dough energetically until it is soft and elastic. It must have the consistency of an earlobe. Cover it with a damp cloth and leave to rise in a warm place sheltered from draughts for about 2 and a half hours.

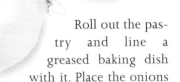

Flour the table or the pastry board again and roll out the dough into a circle or a rectangle with a rolling pin, put the tomatoes on top, squashed with a fork, lightly prick the surface with a fork and leave to rise for twenty more minutes.

Cook in a hot oven for approx. 20 minutes, keeping the temperature around 200-250°C.

Remove from the oven and garnish with a pinch of marjoram or finely chopped basil and the crushed garlic, dribble oil over it and put it into the oven again for 5 minutes before serving.

ONION QUICHE

◆

For the savoury pastry: 230 g of flour, 120 g of butter, 1 egg, salt.
For the filling: 500 g of onions, 3 eggs, paprika, $\frac{1}{2}$ l of milk, 70 g of grated Parmesan cheese, extra virgin olive oil, salt.

Make the flour into a mound on the pastry board, make a well in the centre, place into the well the butter cut into small pieces, a pinch of salt and the yolk of the egg.

Work the dough with the fingers, adding half a glass of warm water, make it into a ball, cover with a cloth and leave it to stand for about half an hour in a cool place, or even in the refrigerator.

Cut the onion into thin slices and put them into a frying pan with a little oil, cover and cook slowly on a low heat (if necessary add a little hot water). When the onions are soft and well cooked, add a little salt and flavour with the paprika, then leave to cool.

Roll out the pastry and line a greased baking dish with it. Place the onions into the pastry case; beat the egg together with the milk, the grated cheese and a pinch of salt, and pour onto the onions. Put into a hot oven (around 220°C) and cook for about half an hour.

SFINCIUNI
◀ Sicily ▶

600 g of risen bread dough, 6 slices of fresh Caciocavallo cheese, 4 anchovy fillets, 6 tomatoes, 3 onions, 1 clove of garlic, 1 basil leaf, 1 spoonful of bread crumbs, extra virgin olive oil, salt, pepper.

Lightly fry the garlic clove in the oil; skin the tomatoes and cut them into small pieces and add them to the contents of the pan, together with the basil leaf; add the anchovy fillets, squashing them so that they break up into pieces.

Add a little salt and pepper, and then add the breadcrumbs.

Roll out the dough and put it onto an oiled oven tray, cover with the sliced onions, the slices of Caciocavallo cheese and the tomato sauce; cook in a hot oven for 15 minutes.

SPINACH STRUDEL

◆

For the putt-pastry: 200 g of flour, 200 g of butter, 1 egg, salt.
For the filling: 700 g of spinach, 50 g raisins, 50 g of pine kernels, 2 eggs, paprika, 100 g of grated Parmesan cheese, extra virgin olive oil, salt.

For the preparation of the pastry use chilled instruments and ice cold water. Add a pinch of salt and a cup of ice cold water to the flour and knead it until the dough is firm; leave to stand, covered with a cloth, in a cool, dark place. With wet fingers, knead the butter until it is the same consistency as the dough, then cut it into a rectangular shape. Roll out the pastry on a well floured work surface and place the butter in the middle; fold the pastry over the butter and press it lightly with the rolling pin so that the butter is incorporated into the dough, then leave to stand for 5 minutes.

Now the pastry must be folded and rolled out, and folded again in order to become fragrant and crumbly. Keep the flour at hand because it is necessary to keep the work surface and the rolling pin well floured. Roll out the pastry into a rectangle 1 cm thick, fold it in three and roll it out again, then fold it again into three in the other direction and roll it out once more, then leave it to stand for 15 minutes in the refrigerator. Then repeat the same operations twice more, including leaving it to stand (it must be folded in three six times in all), after which the pastry is ready.

Clean and wash the spinach carefully and boil it in a little salted water, or steam it. Squeeze it to eliminate the excess liquid and put it into a casserole

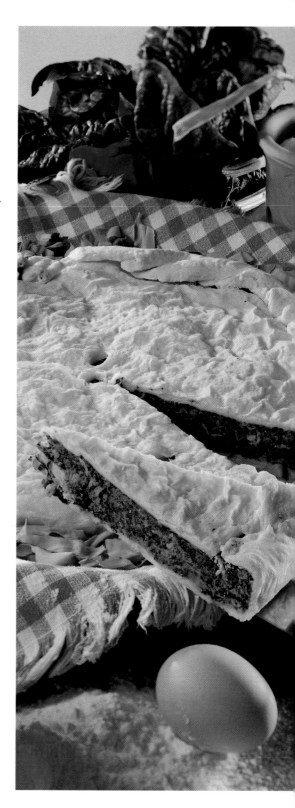

with a little oil, leaving it on a moderate heat until it is dry. If preferred, instead of boiling the spinach can be cooked directly in the casserole with a little oil. Leave it to cool, then put it into a bowl, together with the grated cheese, the raisins previously washed and softened in warm water, the pine kernels and the egg beaten with a pinch of paprika.

Amalgamate all the ingredients and leave to stand so that the flavours are all blended together. Roll out the pastry on a pastry board and place the spinach mixture on top, taking care to leave the edges free. Roll the pastry up to make the typical strudel shape, press the two side edges together, place it on an oiled baking tray and cook in a pre-heated oven for about 40 minutes.

TARALLUCCI BISCUITS
◄ *Calabria* ►

300 g of flour, 2 eggs, 2 spoonfuls of dry white wine, 2 spoonfuls of extra virgin olive oil, salt, hot red pepper.

Work the flour with the eggs, the oil, the white wine, a pinch of pepper and a pinch of salt.

Divide the dough into strips about 10 cm long and fold them into loops, joining the two ends. In a saucepan, bring to the boil abundant salted water and toss in the *Tarallucci* biscuits; as soon as they float to the surface remove them with a perforated spoon and place them on a oiled baking tray. Cook in a hot oven (180°C) for about 20 minutes. The biscuits can be flavoured with fennel seeds and without the pepper; or a spoonful of olive paste and a few chopped olives can be added.

SEMOLINA CAKE
◆

250 g of semolina, 2 eggs, 1 l of milk (or $^{1}/_{2}$ l of milk and $^{1}/_{2}$ l of vegetable broth or water), 150 g of grated Parmesan cheese, extra virgin olive oil, salt.

Bring the milk (or the milk and water or vegetable broth) to the boil then sprinkle in the semolina, stirring continually to avoid the formation of lumps. Add salt and cook for just over 5 minutes, take from the heat, stir in the grated Parmesan cheese, leaving aside a few spoonfuls; leave to cool, then stir in the eggs.

Put the mixture into an oiled oven dish, sprinkle the rest of the Parmesan cheese on top and cook in a hot oven at 220°C for about 20 minutes; then lower the heat and cook for another ten minutes.

SAUCES AND DRESSINGS

GARLIC DRESSING

◆

2 eggs, 4 cloves of garlic, 20 g of pine kernels, extra virgin olive oil, salt, pepper.

Hard boil the eggs and leave to cool; boil the garlic in a little water for a quarter of an hour. Put the hard boiled eggs, the garlic, the pine kernels, two spoonfuls of oil, a pinch of salt and a pinch of pepper into a food mixer; mix until a smooth sauce is produced.

GENOESE *PESTO*
◀ *Liguria* ▶

30 basil leaves, 1 clove of garlic, 1-2 spoonfuls of pine kernels, 1 spoonful of grated sheep's milk cheese, 1 spoonful of grated Parmesan cheese, extra virgin olive oil, salt.

Wash the basil leaves, dry them and work them with a stone pestle and mortar (squashing them with a circular movement against the sides of the mortar, without beating them in the usual way) together with the garlic and the pine kernels; add the grated cheese and a pinch of salt. As soon as the ingredients are well mixed, dilute them (using the pestle in the way of a spoon) with as much oil as necessary in order to produce a stiff cream. The dressing can also be prepared using a food mixer.

Apart from being an excellent sauce for pasta, pesto can also be used on toast, crackers, pastry biscuits and to flavour meat.

GREEN SAUCE

1 large sprig of parsley, 1 clove of garlic, 1 egg, 3 salted anchovies, 2-3 bread rolls, white wine vinegar, 2 glassfuls of extra virgin olive oil, pepper in grains.

Put the soft inner part of the bread into the vinegar. Hard-boil the egg. Remove the salt from the anchovies, bone them and squash them into a paste, mixing them with the yolk of the hard-boiled egg. Make the mixture into a smooth paste, pouring oil onto it little by little while stirring, then add the finely chopped parsley, the crushed garlic and the bread soaked in vinegar, mixing well with a wooden spoon. Add a generous dose of freshly ground pepper. The sauce must be of a semi-liquid consistency, therefore, if necessary, add a little more oil.
There is also a Genoese version, with the addition of capers, pine kernels and green olives, all finely minced.

PEARÀ SAUCE
◀ *Veneto* ▶

80 g of ox bone marrow, 300 g of breadcrumbs, 3 dl of meat broth, salt, pepper in grains.

This sauce must be prepared in a small, deep earthenware bowl; the bread crumbs are obtained by grating stale common bread, not milk bread or any kind of soft bread; the broth, obtained from the cooking of mixed meats, must be filtered and the fat removed.

◆ Place the earthenware bowl on the heat, with a wire net beneath to protect it from the flames, and melt the bone marrow in it. Add the fine bread crumbs and mix in to absorb the fat well.

◆ Add hot broth, mixing carefully to avoid lumps forming; leave to simmer on a low heat for 2-3 hours, stirring occasionally. Before removing from the heat, add salt to taste and abundant freshly ground pepper.

◆ A lesser quantity of bone marrow can be used if melted butter or oil are added to the breadcrumbs. The pepper can also be substituted by freshly grated radish, adding grated Parmesan before removing from the heat.

This sauce is traditionally served with boiled beef: each diner is served with a portion (usually a generous portion) that is placed directly onto the already sliced meat on the plate.

FIRST
COURSES

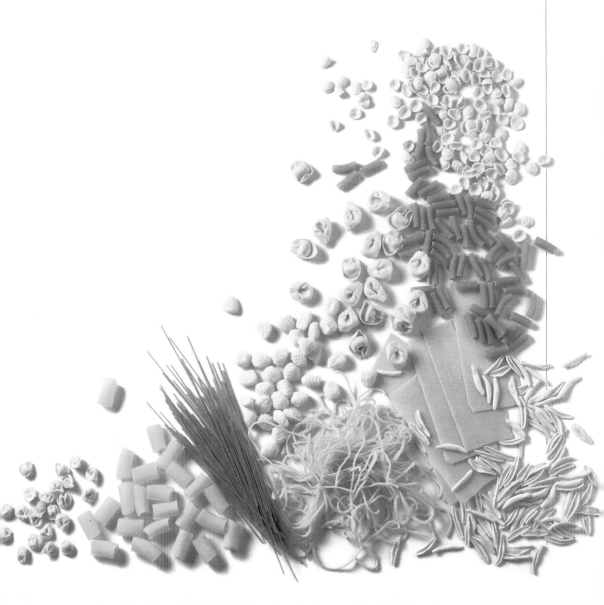

ACQUA COTTA
◀ *Tuscany* ▶ 🔲

2 onions, 2 tomatoes, 1 stick of celery, 1 egg per person, rosemary, extra virgin olive oil, salt, slices of home-made type bread.

This soup, also common in other regions, often has different ingredients just because its main characteristic is that it makes use of the vegetables in season available on hand.
In a lightly oiled earthenware saucepan, cook the sliced onions, celery and fresh tomatoes. After about 30 minutes, add to the vegetables hot water, salt and a few ground rosemary leaves.
While the soup is boiling (5 more minutes are enough), toast the slices of bread and put them in the bowls of the diners, beat the eggs and pour them onto the slices of bread.
Pour the boiling hot soup onto the slices of bread with the beaten egg and serve.

AGNOLOTTI
WITH TRUFFLES
◀ *The Aosta Valley, Piedmont* ▶

For the agnolotti: 400 g of flour, 4 eggs, salt.
For the filling: 150 g of lean pork, 150 g of raw ham, 100 g of veal, 50 g of butter, ¹/₂ a truffle, 1 egg, dry white wine, 1 generous spoonful of grated Parmesan cheese, salt, pepper.
To garnish: ¹/₂ a truffle, grated Parmesan cheese, butter.

Put into a small saucepan the butter, the veal, the pork, the minced ham, half of the truffle – ¹/₂ of a whole truffle – (black or white) cleaned and cut into thin slices with a special instrument, the egg, the Parmesan cheese, salt and pepper. Cook on a low heat, mixing all the ingredients together and adding – only if necessary – a little white wine.
When everything is well cooked prepare the pasta by mixing the ingredients together and kneading it until the dough is firm and the surface shiny.
Flour the work surface and with a rolling pin (and/or with a pasta machine) roll out the dough very thinly. On one half of the dough place little piles of the filling.
Fold the dough in half and cut it with a wheel cutter into the shapes preferred, making little packets, each one containing a little of the filling. Leave the *agnolotti* (the pasta packets) on a cloth but uncovered to dry for about half an hour.
In the meantime, heat a saucepan full of salted water. When it is boiling throw in the *agnolotti*, removing them with when cooked a perforated spoon. Place them on a hot serving plate and sprinkle them with grated Parmesan cheese and melted butter, dusting them with the remaining grated truffle.

NEAPOLITAN AGNOLOTTI
◀ *Campania* ▶ 🔲

For the agnolotti: 400 g of flour, 4 eggs, salt.
For the filling: 300 g of ricotta cheese, 2 eggs, 1 large mozzarella cheese, 1 large sprig of basil leaves, salt, pepper in grains.
For the ragout: 300 g of lean beef, 500 g of tomato pulp, 1 onion, a few basil leaves, red wine, extra virgin olive oil, salt, pepper.

Mix the ingredients for the dough, kneading them to obtain a firm consistency with a shiny surface. In the meantime prepare the filling: mix well together the ricotta cheese, the eggs, the basil and the minced mozzarella, salt and freshly ground pepper. Begin to prepare the ragout: soften the grated onion in an earthenware bowl together with a few spoonfuls of oil, then add the meat cut into very small pieces and brown for a few minutes while stirring; add salt and a little wine; after a few minutes add the tomato pulp.

Cook on a low heat for about an hour, adding the finely chopped basil and the pepper just before removing from the heat.

Roll out the dough on a floured work surface and cut it into large circles; in the middle of each circle place a little of the filling, fold the disc in half to form pockets, pressing the edges well together. Boil the *agnolotti* (the pasta pockets) in abundant salted water, drain and serve garnished with the meat ragout and, if desired, with grated Parmesan (or sheep's milk) cheese.

FISH BROTH
◀ *The Marches* ▶

1.2 of kg mixed fish (dog fish, cod, squills, mullet, etc.), 500 g of cuttlefish, 1 onion, finely chopped parsley, 1 small pinch of saffron, 1 generous glass of dry white wine, 1 spoonful of vine-

gar, 1 glassful of extra virgin olive oil, salt, pepper, croutons.

Clean the fish and cut up the larger ones so that all the pieces are the same size; remove the ink bladder and the bone from the cuttlefish and cut into strips. Wash all the fish in abundant salted water and drain well. Soften the onion in a casserole with the oil; when it is golden, add the cuttlefish and the saffron dissolved in a little hot water. As soon as the cuttlefish become yellow, add salt and pepper and cover with water; leave them to cook slowly for half an hour.

Take a large pan with two handles (to be able to move the fish around without using a spoon or a fork) and place a layer of squills on the bottom, if you are using this fish, then the cooked cuttlefish and the pieces of the tougher kinds of fish, and on top of these place the more delicate kinds; pour the hot liquid in which the cuttlefish were cooked into the pan. When everything is placed in the pan, cover the fish almost completely with wine, vinegar and hot water, in more or less equal quantities; add salt and pepper to taste and cook on a high heat for a quarter of an hour, shaking the pan from time to time. Serve the soup piping hot with toasted croutons.

BUCATINI ALL'AMATRICIANA
◀ Lazio ▶

400 g of bucatini pasta, 200 g of lean pig cheek or lean un-smoked bacon, 300 g of firm ripe tomatoes, $^{1}/_{2}$ onion, grated sheep's milk cheese, extra virgin olive oil, salt, paprika.

Cut the pork into cubes and brown them in a few spoonfuls of oil: as soon as the fat has melted, take it out of the pan and put aside. In the liquid remaining in the pan, lightly brown the grated onion, then add the tomatoes (tossed for a moment into boiling water to remove the skins) from which the seeds have been removed and which have been cut into strips. Add salt and cook gently for about ten minutes to reduce the liquid. Add the pork again to finish cooking and flavour with the paprika.
Boil the bucatini pasta in abundant salted water, draining when still firm. Garnish the pasta with the pork sauce and with a generous sprinkling of grated sheep's milk cheese.
Originally this recipe did not include tomato, therefore it can also be prepared without the tomato or with very little.

45

BUCATINI WITH LAMB SAUCE
◀ Abruzzo, Molise ▶

400 g of bucatini pasta, 200 g of lamb, 2 cloves of garlic, 1 branch of rosemary, 2 bay leaves, 400 g of tomato pulp, red wine, grated sheep's milk cheese, extra virgin olive oil, salt, pepper.

Cut the lamb into small pieces and brown them in abundant oil together with the garlic (which must be removed as soon as it begins to brown), the rosemary and the bay leaves.
Add a little wine and let this evaporate. Add the tomato pulp, salt and pepper and finish cooking on a low heat.

In the meantime, boil the bucatini pasta in abundant salted water, drain and mix with the sauce, then sprinkle with the grated sheep's milk cheese.

CANEDERLI
(BACON BALLS)
◀ Trentino-Alto Adige ▶

400 g of stale bread without the crust, 100 g of smoked bacon, 50 g of salami, 1 1/2 l of broth, 2 eggs, white flour, milk, a sprig of parsley, extra virgin olive oil, grated Parmesan cheese, salt.

Cut the bread into cubes and dampen with the milk, without letting them absorb too much; squeeze them delicately. Cook the bacon and the salami, cut into cubes, gently in a little oil, then mix in the bread cubes a little flour, the finely chopped parsley and the eggs. Add salt and mix well together to form a firm smooth paste; make it into balls as big as a mandarin. Bring the broth to the boil, then simmer on a low heat and cook the canederli balls for about 20 minutes, until they rise to the surface. Serve the canederli in the hot meat broth or, if preferred, dry and garnished with tomato sauce or, with melted butter and grated Parmesan cheese.

BAKED CANNELLONI

◆

12 cannelloni, 500 g of spinach, 250 g of ricotta cheese, 2 eggs, nutmeg, grated Parmesan cheese, butter, salt, pepper.

Clean and wash the spinach in a little salted water, drain and squeeze them to eliminate the liquid and mince them. In a bowl, mash the ricotta cheese with a fork and amalgamate it with the spinach, the egg yolks and a few spoonfuls of Parmesan cheese; flavour with salt, pepper and grated nutmeg. If this paste is too dry, add the egg whites or a drop of milk. Fill the cannelloni with the paste; place them on an oven tray on which has been spread a little béchamel sauce. Spread the rest of the sauce over the cannelloni and sprinkle with Parmesan and a few knobs of butter; put into a hot oven to brown.
Remove from oven and leave to stand for a few minutes before serving.

CAPPELLETTI
(PASTA IN BROTH)
◀ Emilia Romagna ▶ 📷

<u>For the broth</u>: 500 g of beef, 500 g of veal, 1/2 chicken, 1 onion, 1 carrot, 1 stick of celery, 1 tomato, cloves, 1 bay leaf, salt, pepper in grains.
<u>For the cappelletti</u>: 400 g of flour, 4 eggs, salt.
<u>For the filling</u>: 100 g of chicken breast, 100 g of pork loin, 100 g of veal, 150 g of raw ham, 1 slice of Bologna sausage, 100 g of grated Parmesan cheese, 2 eggs, nutmeg, butter, salt, pepper.

First prepare a good broth: clean and scorch the chicken and place it with the other meats in a saucepan in 1 1/2 litres of cold salted water. Cook on a moderate heat; as soon as the water comes to the boil, add the vegetables (with 1-2 cloves stuck into the onion), a few grains of pepper and the bay leaf. Leave to boil gently for about an hour and a half, removing the froth from time to time. When cooked, remove the meat from the broth and filter out the remains of the vegeta-

bles. Leave to cool, then with a wooden spoon, remove the rest of the fat that will come to the surface and solidify.

Cook the meat with a little butter in a pan. Mince together the raw ham and the Bologna sausage; amalgamate this with the eggs, the grated Parmesan cheese, a pinch of grated nutmeg, and salt and pepper. Prepare the pastry, mixing together all the ingredients and working it until the dough is firm and with a shiny surface. Flour the work surface and roll out the dough thinly with a rolling pin (or a special pasta machine); cut the dough into small squares. Place a little of the filling on each square. Fold the squares into triangles, fold each triangle around a finger and press the ends together, turning the corner outwards. Cook the *cappelletti* pasta in the meat broth and serve with a sprinkling of grated Parmesan cheese.

RADISH PANCAKES

◆

<u>For the pancake batter</u>: 100 g of white flour, 2 dl of milk, 3 eggs, salt and pepper.
<u>For the filling</u>: 600 g of radishes, 1 onion, béchamel sauce, dry white wine, grated Parmesan cheese, butter, olive oil, salt, pepper in grains.

Put the flour in a bowl. Add the milk gradually, mixing well with a wooden spoon or with a whisk, so that lumps do not form. Add a pinch of salt and one of pepper, and beat well. Leave the batter to stand. Heat the pancake hot-plate (or use a lightly greased anti-adhesive frying pan 15 cm in diameter). Pour two spoonfuls of the batter onto the plate and, cook on both sides, turning it over with a spatula.

Cut the onion into thin slices; wash the radishes well and cut them into thin strips; lightly fry the onion and the radishes in a pan with a few spoonfuls of oil.

Pour a little white wine on, add salt, and a sprinkling of freshly ground pepper, and, turning down the heat, continue cooking for ten minutes. Mix half of the béchamel into the boiled radishes. Put this mixture onto the pancakes, fold them into four, and place in a buttered oven dish, one half overlaying the other.

Pour the rest of the béchamel onto the pancakes, and sprinkle with grated Parmesan cheese and a few knobs of butter and replace in the oven to brown.

POTATO *CULINGIONIS*
◀ *Sardinia* ▶

<u>For the dough</u>: 500 g of flour, lard, salt.
<u>For the filling</u>: 600 g of potatoes, 300 g of grated strong sheep's milk cheese, 2 cloves of garlic, a few mint leaves, salt.
<u>For the sauce</u>: 300 g of tomato purée, 100 g of grated mature sheep's milk cheese.

Make a mound with the flour with a well in the centre, add the lard and

enough water to form a soft dough; work the dough well, then cover with a cloth and leave to stand for a time.

Boil the potatoes, peel them and mash them in a large bowl; add the grated sheep's milk cheese, a few mint leaves, the crushed garlic and salt to taste.

Roll out the dough thinly and cut out discs with a diameter of about 7 cm. Place a little of the potato mixture in the centre of each disc, fold over and seal, pinching the edges to form a shape similar to an ear of corn.

Cook the *culingionis* in abundant salted water, drain and place in an ovenproof dish; cover with the hot tomato sauce and the grated mature sheep's milk cheese. Place in a moderate oven for about ten minutes before serving.

FETTUCCINE ALLA ROMANA (ROMAN STYLE NOODLES)
◀ *Lazio* ▶

400 g of fettuccine pasta, 500 g of firm ripe tomatoes, 300 g of beef, 1 onion, 1 carrot, 1 stick of celery, paprika, $\frac{1}{2}$ glass of red wine, 1 spoonful of lard, salt.

Put the tomatoes in boiling water for a moment, remove the skins and the seeds, then squash them to a pulp. Lightly fry the finely chopped onion, carrot and celery in the lard, then add the beef, cut into small pieces, sprinkle with salt and pepper.

Pour over the wine and let this evaporate, then add the tomato pulp. Add salt to taste, then heat up again and cook this sauce. Boil the *fettuccine* in salted water, remove when still firm, drain, garnish with the sauce and serve.

FUSILLI PASTA WITH BROAD BEANS
◀ Basilicata ▶

400 g of fusilli pasta, 400 g of firm ripe tomatoes, 2 cloves of garlic, a few basil leaves, extra virgin olive oil, salt, paprika.

Put the tomatoes in boiling water for a moment, remove the skins and the seeds, then squash them to a pulp. Clean the broad beans, eliminating the black eyes. Lightly fry the crushed garlic in a few spoonfuls of oil; add the beans.
Cook for a few minutes to absorb the flavour, then add the tomato pulp. Add salt to taste and a pinch of paprika, and continue cooking on a moderate heat, adding a little hot water from time to time; before removing from the heat, add the chopped basil leaves. Boil the pasta in abundant salted water, remove from the heat when still firm and garnish with the bean sauce and a dribble of uncooked oil.

GNOCCHI ALLA VALDOSTANA (AOSTA VALLEY DUMPLINGS)
◀ The Aosta Valley, Piedmont ▶

200 g of coarse maize flour, 100 g of fine maize flour, 150 g of Fontina cheese, 2 eggs, 1 l of milk, nutmeg, grated Parmesan cheese, butter, salt, pepper.

Put the milk into a saucepan and bring almost to the boil. At this point add the flours and a pinch of salt and cook, stirring continuously as for a normal polenta (maize porridge).
When it is cooked (after about 40 minutes) add the Fontina cheese cut into small cubes, a spoonful of butter and a pinch of grated nutmeg, stirring well to amalgamate the ingredients.
Leave to cool, then add the 2 egg yolks. Roll out this dough on a flat surface to a thickness of 1 cm.
When the dough is cold, cut out circles using a glass with a diameter of 4 or 5 cm and place the discs in a buttered rectangular ovenproof dish, slightly overlapping one another.
Dust with grated Parmesan cheese and pepper, dribble a little melted butter on top and brown in a hot oven for about ten minutes before serving.

POTATO GNOCCHI (DUMPLINGS)
◀ Veneto ▶

For the dumplings: 1 kg of potatoes, 200 g of flour, a few sage leaves, butter, salt.
For the sauce: 800 g of firm ripe tomatoes, 1 sprig of basil, 1/2 spoonful of sugar, extra virgin olive oil, salt, pepper.

Boil the potatoes, peel them and mash when still hot with a potato masher, allowing them to fall onto a pastry board, or clean work surface. Work with the hands, incorporating as much flour as necessary to obtain the correct consistency (the dumplings will be tender if they are prepared with only a little flour, and using the right kind of potatoes). With this dough, form long cylinders as big as a finger, cut them into short pieces, and give them the characteristic gnocchi shape by pulling them across the underside of a grater with the forefinger. Prepare the tomato sauce: wash the tomatoes and put them in boiling water for a moment in order to peel them easily, remove any green parts where they were attached to the plant, then mince them with a vegetable mincer. If they contain too much liquid, leave them to drain on a sloping surface for at least a quarter of an hour before mincing them. Put the tomato purée in a pan with a little oil and cook on a moderate heat for about 30 minutes, to reduce the liquid, then add salt and sugar. Just before removing from the heat flavour with pepper and the finely chopped basil.

Separately, melt a generous amount of butter in a pan, flavouring it with a few sage leaves. Bring an abundant quantity of salted water to the boil in a large saucepan, then throw in the gnocchi, a few at a time. As soon as they float to the surface, remove them at once with a perforated spoon and place them on the diners' plates, garnishing them with the tomato sauce and the melted butter.

Alternatively to the tomato sauce, the gnocchi can also be served with meat ragout, Gorgonzola cheese, or even with melted butter and cinnamon.

JOTA
◀ Friuli-Venezia Giulia ▶

500 g of sauerkraut, 200 g of dry Borlotti beans, 2 potatoes, 2 spoonfuls of flour, 300 g of un-smoked bacon, 2 bay leaves, 1 pinch of cumin seeds, 1/2 glass of extra virgin olive oil, salt, pepper.

Leave the beans to soak in water overnight and the next day boil them in fresh water. After about an hour add the potatoes, peeled and cut into rather large pieces. In the meantime, fry the flour in the oil, taking care that it does not burn; when it is dark, add the sauerkraut, the bacon cut into small cubes, the cumin seeds, the bay leaves, and the salt and pepper. Cover with water and cook until the liquid has evaporated. Put the sauerkraut in the saucepan with the beans and potatoes and continue cooking for another 20 minutes, stirring from time to time. Add salt to taste.

Before serving, leave this jota to stand for a while; it is even better if it can be prepared the day before.

BAKED LASAGNE
◀ Emilia Romagna ▶

For the lasagne: 400 g of flour, 4 eggs, salt.
For the béchamel sauce: 50 g of butter, 50 g of flour, 1/2 l of milk, nutmeg, salt, pepper.
For the sauce: 150 g of minced beef, 1 slice of cooked ham weighing 50 g, 50 g of sausage, 300 g of tomato pulp, 1/2 onion, 1/2 carrot, 1/2 stick of celery, 1 clove garlic, a few bay, sage and basil leaves, 1 clove, cinnamon, 1/2 glass of red wine, extra virgin olive oil, salt, pepper.
Between the layers: 2 mozzarella cheeses, grated Parmesan cheese, butter, salt.

Prepare the pasta dough, mixing the ingredients and working them until the dough is firm with a shiny surface. Flour the work surface and roll out the dough very thinly with a rolling pin (and/or with a pasta machine), cut it into rectangles 8 x 16 cm. Bring abundant salted water to the boil and cook the pasta for a few minutes, drain and place for a moment in a pan of cold water in order to prevent further cooking, then lay out to dry between clean cloths.

Prepare the sauce: clean and grate the onion, carrot, celery and garlic; mince the ham. Lightly fry the sausage in a little oil, then add the minced and grated vegetables and ham, mixing well to amalgamate the ingredients, and cooking them until they are soft. Before they begin to turn brown, add the minced beef and cook until all the ingredients are uniformly coloured; add the wine and let it evaporate, then add the tomato, the bay leaves, the other herbs and spices, and salt. Lower the heat, cover the pan and leave to simmer for about an hour: the sauce must be liquid enough to dampen well the layers of pasta.

In the meantime, prepare the béchamel: melt the butter in a casserole on a low heat and, with the aid of a wooden spoon, amalgamate this with the flour. At this point (using a whisk instead of the spoon, if preferred) dilute with the milk, which should be hot but not brought to boiling point. The milk must be added little by little, stirring all the time: only in this way is it possible to avoid lumps forming. Continue to mix steadily all the time, until the sauce begins to thicken; from the moment the first bubbles appear at boiling point, count ten minutes of cooking time. Continue to mix and before removing from the heat, add salt, pepper and a pinch of grated nutmeg.

If a thicker sauce is needed, the doses of butter and flour can be increased (but they must always be the same quantity as each other), while the quantity of milk remains the same, or

you can allow the sauce to become thicker, cooking it for a little longer.

Spread a little meat sauce and a little béchamel sauce on the bottom of an oiled rectangular baking tray, mixing them with a wooden spoon. Place a first layer of lasagne in the tray and cover with mozzarella cheese cut into cubes and some grated Parmesan cheese; make another layer of pasta, covering it with the meat sauce and the béchamel sauce. Continue in this way, alternating the ingredients between the layers of pasta, until the ingredients are finished, with meat sauce and béchamel on top. Dust the top with grated Parmesan cheese, placing a few knobs of butter here and there, and leave in a hot oven for about 40 minutes; remove from the oven and serve.

MACARONI WITH RICOTTA CHEESE AND SAUSAGE
◀ Calabria ▶

51

400 g of macaroni, 400 g of fresh ricotta cheese, 200 g of sausage, grated sheep's milk cheese, salt, pepper in grains.

Remove the skin from the sausage, break it up and cook lightly on a low heat in a pan with a little water, without browning it. In a soup bowl, mash the ricotta cheese with a wooden fork, then add the sausage and abundant freshly ground pepper.

Boil the pasta in abundant salted water, remove when still firm, and drain, leaving a little of the cooking water, however; add the ricotta and sausage mixture and sprinkle with a generous amount of grated sheep's milk cheese.

MALLOREDDUS
◀ Sardinia ▶

250 g of extra fine flour, 150 g of white flour, saffron, salt.

Mix the extra fine flour with the ordinary white flour and make a mound with a well in the centre on the pastry board; pour a cup and a half of warm water into the centre with a few pinches of saffron dissolved in the water; add a pinch of salt and mix well.

When the dough is smooth, shape it into thin cylinders, cut the cylinders into pieces a couple of centimetres long, press these malloreddus against the special instrument or against the back of a grater, to give them their characteristic grooved appearance. Spread them on a tray and leave them to dry out: malloreddus must be quite dry before cooking, so it is advisable to prepare them a couple of days in advance.

They can be served with a sheep's milk cheese sauce or a potato sauce

MILLE COSEDDE
◀ Calabria ▶

350 g of short pasta, 150 g of dried broad beans, 150 g of dried chick peas, ½ Savoy cabbage, 1 onion, 1 carrot, 1 stick of celery, 50 g of smoked bacon, grated sheep's milk cheese, extra virgin olive oil, salt, pepper, paprika.

Leave the legumes to soak for 24 hours; the following day, drain them and cook them in fresh water (add salt when they have finished cooking).

Clean the Savoy cabbage, and cut it into thin pieces. Grate the carrot, the onion and the celery and mince the bacon and lightly fry these in plenty of oil.

Keeping the heat moderate, add the drained legumes, the Savoy cabbage and 2 litres of water, add salt to taste and flavour with the paprika.

When it begins to boil, add the pasta. When it is cooked, serve with generous quantities of grated sheep's milk cheese.

CHESTNUT AND MILK SOUP
◀ The Aosta Valley ▶

250 g of dried shelled chestnuts, pine kernels, raisins, 1 ½ l of milk, salt.

Leave the dried chestnuts to soak for a whole day in warm water. Drain them and boil in water for about 2 hours, adding salt just before removing from the heat. Drain them again and continue cooking them in milk for another 45 minutes, adding salt to taste and a spoonful of raisins and one of pine kernels, previously softened in a little warm water, and then squeezed out.

52

Increase the heat for a moment just before serving this delicious energy giving soup.

BARLEY SOUP

◆ 🔳

300 g of barley, 150 g of dried beans, 1 ham bone, 2 potatoes, 2 carrots, 1 onion, 1 stick of celery, 1 bunch of parsley, grated Parmesan cheese, extra virgin olive oil, salt.

Soak the ham bone and the dried beans in separate bowls for two hours. Drain the beans and cook on a low heat for another 2 hours. Soak the barley for 24 hours, rinse it under running water, cover with fresh water and boil this for a couple of hours. Lightly fry the thinly sliced onion and the finely chopped parsley and celery in oil; add them to the barley – just as it begins to boil – together with the potatoes and the sliced carrots, the drained ham bone, salt and sufficient hot water. When cooked, add the boiled beans and remove the ham bone. Serve the soup with grated Parmesan cheese.

SARDINIAN VEGETABLE SOUP
◀ *Sardinia* ▶

1½ kg of seasonal vegetables, 200 g of malloreddus (see recipe above), wild fennel, extra virgin olive oil, salt, pepper in grains.

Clean, wash and cut into small pieces all the vegetables; put them in a saucepan and cover with cold water. Add the finely chopped sprig of wild fennel, salt and freshly ground pepper. Cook for about one and a half hours; 30 minutes before the cooking is finished, add the *malloreddus*. Serve with a dribble of raw oil.

TUSCAN VEGETABLE SOUP
◄ *Tuscany* ►

300 g of small pasta, 250 g of fresh beans, 150 g of beetroot, 1 slice of smoked bacon, $^1/_2$ Savoy cabbage, $^1/_2$ black cabbage, 3 tomatoes, 2 leeks, 2 carrots, 1 onion, 1 stick of celery, 1 clove of garlic, basil, extra virgin olive oil, salt, pepper.

Boil the beans in salted water, drain them, putting the water aside, and mash half of them in a vegetable masher or food mixer.
Put the garlic, celery, onion, carrots, basil and bacon cut into cubes in a few spoonfuls of oil and fry lightly.
Add the vegetables cut into small cubes and the beans – both whole and mashed – and the cooking liquid of the beans. Add more hot water, salt and pepper and boil for half an hour on a low heat. Add small pasta, cooked separately, before serving, or, if preferred serve the vegetable soup with slices of bread toasted in the oven.

ORECCHIETTE WITH TURNIP HEADS
◄ *Puglia* ►

For the orecchiette: 350 g of white flour, 100 g of very fine durum wheat flour, salt.

For the sauce: 300 g of turnip heads, 2 cloves of garlic, 1 spoonful of raisins (optional), 1 spoonful of pine kernels (optional), 2 salted anchovies, grated sheep's milk cheese, extra virgin olive oil, salt, paprika.

To prepare the *orecchiette*, make a mound of the ordinary flour mixed with the extra fine flour and a pinch of salt on a floured work surface. Add enough tepid water to obtain a firm dough and work the dough until it is smooth. After about 10 minutes, divide the dough and roll it with the hands to form long cylinders a couple of centimetres wide; cut the cylinders into pieces about 1 cm long. Flatten them against the work surface to give them the shape of round shells. Place the thumb on each shell and fold the edge backwards, to form the shape of an ear. Lay them to dry on a floured cloth.
Wash the turnip heads thoroughly and boil them in abundant salted water, removing from the heat when they are still firm. Drain but keep to one side the cooking water. Lightly fry the crushed garlic with a few spoonfuls of oil, then add the de-salted anchovies, breaking them up in the pan. Add the turnip heads and bring to cooking point (add a little salted water, if necessary); just before removing from the heat, check the salt and add the paprika, the pine kernels and the raisins, previously softened in a little warm water, drained and dried. Boil the orecchiette using the water in which the

turnip heads were cooked; remove from the heat and drain while they are still firm; stir them gently in the pan together with the turnip tops and serve garnished with grated sheep's milk cheese, or cut into small cubes if the cheese is fresh.

COOKED BREAD
◀ *Liguria* ▶

400 g of stale bread, 1 ¹/₂ of l of meat broth, butter, grated Parmesan cheese, 2 eggs.
<u>For the broth</u>: 500 g of beef, 500 g of veal, ¹/₂ chicken, 1 onion, 1 carrot, 1 stick of celery, 1 tomato, 1-2 cloves, 1 bay leaf, salt, pepper in grains.

For the broth, clean and scorch the chicken and put it with the other meats in a large saucepan with 1¹/₂ litres of cold water and a handful of salt. Cook on a moderate heat and, as soon as it begins to boil, add the vegetables (with the clove stuck into the onion), a few grains of pepper and the bay leaf.
Leave it to simmer for about an hour and a half, removing the froth frequently. When it has finished cooking, remove the meat from the broth and filter out the vegetables. To completely remove the fat, leave it to cool, then remove the fat that will come to the surface and solidify, with a wooden spatula. Put the broth into a casserole, together with the stale bread cut into small cubes and a knob of butter, and boil for about ten minutes. Remove from the heat and stir in

the egg yolks, and then flavour with plenty of grated Parmesan cheese.

HAZELNUT *PANSOTTI*
◀ *Liguria* ▶

<u>For the pansotti</u>: 500 g of flour, 3 eggs.
<u>For the filling</u>: 300 g of ricotta cheese, 500 g of beetroot, 500 g of preboggion (cabbage, beetroot and parsley), 1 sprig of borage, 3 eggs, 50 g Parmesan cheese, nutmeg, salt.
<u>For the sauce</u>: hazelnuts, pine kernels, 1 clove of garlic, extra virgin olive oil.

Clean and wash the vegetables and mince them. In a bowl, mix them together the ricotta cheese, the grated Parmesan cheese, the eggs, salt and some grated nutmeg; when mixed well together, add the minced vegetables. To prepare the sauce, mince the hazelnuts, pine kernels and crush the garlic, then work together with a pestle and mortar, gradually dribbling in as much oil as necessary to form a smooth, thick sauce.
To prepare the pasta, roll out the dough thinly and cut it into pieces 5 cm square.

55

Put in the centre of each square a little pile of the filling, fold the square over, and press down the edges to close the little packet. Cook these *pansotti* in boiling salted water, drain them and place them on a heated serving plate, cover them with the hazelnut sauce and serve immediately.

PANZANELLA
◀ *Tuscany* ▶

400 g of stale Tuscan bread cooked in a wood fired oven, 3 ripe tomatoes, 1 red onion, 1 cucumber, 6 basil leaves, 1 spoonful of vinegar, 3 spoonfuls of extra virgin olive oil, salt, pepper in grains.

Dampen the bread with a little water and, while it is softening, peel and slice the cucumber, sprinkling it with a little salt and squeezing it under a heavy upside down plate to extract its liquid. Cut the onion and the tomato into thin slices, and tear up the basil leaves by hand.
Squeeze the bread and crumble it into a bowl, rinse the salt from the cucumber and put it with the bread and all the other vegetables; dress with vinegar, oil, salt and freshly ground pepper; mix delicately and leave to stand in a cool place for at least 10 minutes before serving.

PAPPA AL POMODORO
◀ *Tuscany* ▶

600 g of skinned tomatoes, 300 g of stale Tuscan bread, 1 leek, 1 clove of garlic, 6 basil leaves, ¹/₂ l of meat cube broth, ¹/₂ l of extra virgin olive oil, salt, pepper in grains.

Put into a casserole the roughly minced tomatoes, the bread broken into pieces, the basil leaves, the roughly minced leek, the garlic clove, three spoonfuls of oil, the broth, salt and freshly ground pepper. Bring to the boil and cook, stirring frequently, till the broth has boiled down to half the quantity and the bread has become semi-solid in consistency. Remove from the heat and cover, and leave to stand for at least 15 minutes. Remove the garlic clove. Dribble a little un-cooked oil and grate a generous portion of black pepper onto each serving.
An alternative method is to lightly fry the garlic with the basil and then add the tomatoes, before adding the hot broth and the bread.

NOODLES WITH HARE
◀ *Tuscany* ▶ 🍽

400 g of fresh noodles, 1 boned hare, 1 slice of raw ham of approx. 50 g, 100g of tomato purée, 1 onion, 1 carrot, 1 stick of celery, 1 bay leaf, 1 spoonful of minced parsley, rosemary and thyme, 4 juniper berries, 1 glass of red wine, broth, extra virgin olive oil, salt, pepper.

Lightly fry all the herbs and the finely chopped vegetables and, when the onion begins to colour, add the ham and the hare meat cut into small pieces. Stir around, to blend the flavours, then pour over the red wine, and let it evaporate.
When the meat begins to dry out a little, pour on the tomato purée and continue cooking on a low heat for about an hour and a half, keeping the sauce moist by adding a little hot

broth (or, if preferred, a little milk). Cook the noodles in abundant salted boiling water, drain when they are still firm, and serve in a pre-heated soup bowl with the sauce and garnished with the pieces of meat placed on the surface.

PASTA ALLA NORMA
◀ Sicily ▶

400 g of pasta, 100 g of salted ricotta cheese, 4 aubergines, 500 g of tomato pulp, 1 onion, 40 g of fresh pork fat, extra virgin olive oil, salt, pepper.

To prepare the sauce, put into a pan the fresh pork fat in pieces, the sliced onion and a few spoonfuls of oil; fry lightly, then add the tomato pulp, salt and pepper. Cook on a moderate heat for 20 minutes. In the meantime, slice the aubergines, dust them with salt and leave them for half an hour to release their bitter liquid. Wash and dry them, then fry them in hot oil, remove them with a perforated spoon, and leave them to drain on absorbent paper, then sprinkle them with salt.
Cook the pasta in boiling salted water, remove and drain it when it is still firm, add the tomato sauce and a scattering of crumbled salted ricotta cheese. Garnish the single portions with the fried aubergines and serve immediately.

PASTA AND CHICK PEAS
◀ Lazio ▶

300 g of small pasta, 200 g of chickpeas, 5 cloves of garlic, 4 ripe tomatoes, 1 sprig of rosemary, a few anchovy fillets, extra virgin olive oil, salt, pepper in grains.

Leave the chickpeas to soak in warm water for about 24 hours. Drain them and put them in a saucepan with 3 whole garlic cloves and the rosemary sprig, and cover with fresh water. Add salt and pepper and cook on a low heat for about 3 hours.
In the meantime, lightly brown in a frying pan the other garlic cloves, the roughly minced, peeled de-seeded tomatoes (having removed the skins after tossing them in a saucepan of boiling water for a moment), and the anchovy fillets cut into pieces.
When the chickpeas are cooked, pour the sauce into the saucepan, adding warm water, if necessary, and add the pasta as soon as it comes back to the boil.
Before serving, remove the rosemary and the garlic, sprinkle with freshly ground pepper, and dribble with a little raw oil.

PASTA AND BEANS
◀ Veneto ▶ 📷

200 g of noodles, 300 g of dried Borlotti beans, 1 carrot, 1 onion, 1 stick of celery, 1 clove of garlic, 1 branch of rosemary or sage, 100 g of pork rind, grated cheese, $1/_2$ glass of extra virgin olive oil, salt, pepper.

Scald the pork rind in boiling water for 5 minutes, drain and scrape it well to eliminate all the hairs. Leave the beans to soak for 12 hours.
Clean and wash the vegetables and mince them together with the garlic, the rosemary (or sage, or both) and

lightly fry them in a casserole. After soaking, drain the beans and add them to the casserole.

Leave to stand for a short time for the flavours to be absorbed, then add the drained beans, the pork rind and about $1^1/_2$ litres of salted water, cover and cook on a low heat for about 2-3 hours.

Depending on whether the soup is preferred thicker or thinner, remove some of the beans (one third or one half) and mince them in the food mincer, then put back in the casserole and put them back on the heat.

Put the noodles to cook in the soup and, if it is too dry, add a couple of ladlefuls of hot water.

Before serving remove the pork rind and cut it into thin strips, and place these on the bottom of the soup plates of the diners. Serve the soup with generous quantities of freshly ground pepper, a dribble of raw oil and a powdering of grated cheese.

This is only one of the many versions of pasta and beans common in Italy. This soup can also be flavoured with a little tomato purée or tomato concentrate, and the noodles can be substituted by a mixture of left-over pastas, or the rind can be left out, and so on.

MACARONI HASH

400 g of macaroni, 200 g of mushrooms, 100 g of Emmental cheese, 1 clove of garlic, parsley, béchamel sauce, 100 g grated Parmesan cheese, butter, extra virgin olive oil, salt, pepper.

Clean the mushrooms, slice them and fry them lightly in a little oil already flavoured with the crushed garlic clove; when cooked, remove the garlic and add salt, pepper and finely chopped parsley.

Mix into the béchamel sauce the Emmental cheese cut into small cubes and two spoonfuls of the fried mushrooms.

Cook the pasta in boiling salted water, drain well when it is still firm, and add the mushrooms, then arrange in layers on a baking tray alternating béchamel and grated Parmesan between the layers. Finish with a topping of béchamel, Parmesan and a few knobs of butter; brown the topping in a hot oven for 15 minutes.

PENNE ALL'ARRABBIATA (PEPPERY PEN PASTA)
◀ Calabria ▶

400 g of pen shaped pasta, 500 g of firm ripe tomatoes, 2 cloves of garlic, 1 red peppercorn, grated sheep's milk cheese, extra virgin olive oil, salt.

Place the tomatoes in boiling water for a few moments, then remove the skins and the seeds and roughly mince them. Lightly brown the garlic in a few

spoonfuls of oil; add the tomato pulp. Let the liquid of the sauce evaporate a bit, then add salt and some chopped peppercorn; cook on a moderate heat for about 20 minutes, stirring every now and then.

In the meantime, boil the pasta for about 20 minutes in abundant boiling salted water; remove from the heat and drain when it is still firm.

Place it into the pan with the spicy sauce, stirring over a high heat, and serve garnished with a generous helping of grated sheep's milk cheese.

PIZZOCCHERI (BAKED PASTA)
◀ Lombardy ▶

300 g of pizzoccheri pasta, 150 g of grated Parmesan cheese, 150 g of soft cheese like Fontina or Bitto, 200 g of cabbage or beetroot, 200 g of potatoes, 3 cloves of garlic, 1 sage branch, 100 g of butter, extra virgin olive oil, salt.

Wash and cut the cabbage and the potatoes into pieces, and cook them in abundant salted boiling water; in the same saucepan, cook the pizzoccheri pasta, calculating the timing so that it is all firm when removed from the water and drained.

In the meantime, cut the soft cheese into thin strips and melt the butter with a few spoonfuls of oil, flavoured with the sage and the crushed garlic (to be removed as soon as they are browned). In an ovenproof dish, place a layer of pasta mixed with the vegetables, cover with a layer

of grated Parmesan and the pieces of soft cheese together with the sage and garlic flavoured butter. Continue with another layer of pasta, and so on, until the ingredients are used up, finishing with a generous sprinkling of Parmesan cheese and a few knob of butter. Place in a hot oven for about 10 minutes until the top is browned.

An alternative version of this recipe is to omit the last phase; the pasta and the vegetables are simply mixed with the cheese and the melted butter and brought immediately to the table.

PASTA SQUARES IN BROTH WITH CHICKEN LIVERS
◀ *Emilia Romagna* ▶ 📷

200 g of egg pasta squares, 150 g of chicken livers, 1 l of meat broth, 3 eggs, 1 clove of garlic, 4 sage leaves, 60 g of butter, rosemary, 50 g of grated Parmesan cheese, salt.

Squares of pasta made with egg are available nowadays in all the shops, while in the past they were made with the left-overs of the pasta dough after making *tagliatelle* (noodles) or *cappelletti*

(little hats). Clean the chicken livers well and brown them in a frying pan with 20 g of butter, the garlic and the sage leaves.

Remove from the heat, chop them finely, remove the garlic and the sage leaves from the frying pan and replace the chicken livers with the remains of the butter, the rosemary and a pinch of salt.

Bring the broth to the boil in a saucepan, pour the livers into it, cook for 2 minutes, then add the pasta squares that will cook in just a few minutes. Mix with a wooden spoon, and serve with grated Parmesan cheese sprinkled on top.

RICOTTA RAVIOLI
◆

<u>For the ravioli</u>: 400 g of flour, 4 eggs, salt.
<u>For the filling</u>: 200 g of fresh Roman ricotta (low fat cottage cheese), 2 eggs, nutmeg, grated Parmesan cheese, salt.

To make the pasta, work the flour with the eggs until the dough has a firm consistency and a shiny surface. Flour the work surface and roll out the dough thinly with a rolling pin (and/or a pasta machine).

Break the eggs into a bowl, beat them and add the mashed ricotta, mix well to obtain a smooth paste.

When the filling is ready, lay little heaps at equal distances from each other on one half of the very thinly rolled out dough.

Fold over the other half of the pasta and with a special cutter (or with a wheel cutter) cut out the *ravioli* around the little heaps of filling, in whatever shape you prefer. It is useful

to brush egg white onto the pasta between the little heaps (or you can just dampen it with warm water), so that the edges of each little pasta packet stick together well when it is folded over and cut.

Place the ravioli on a cloth and leave to stand in a cool place for one day; cook them in salted boiling water. After removing them and draining them, garnish them with melted butter and grated Parmesan cheese.

RIBOLLITA
◀ Tuscany ▶

500 g of stale bread, 150 g of dry white beans, 250 g of ripe tomatoes, 1 carrot, ¹/₂ cabbage, 1 potato, 1 onion, 2 cloves of garlic, 1 stick of celery, a few bunches of parsley, thyme, extra virgin olive oil, salt, paprika.

This is also a typically Tuscan dish, with several variations, depending also on the season and therefore the availability of the ingredients. First prepare a good bean soup: leave the beans to soak for 12 hours, then drain them and boil them in fresh water, on a low heat, and in a covered saucepan. In the meantime gently fry the sliced onion, carrot and celery, and the crushed garlic in the oil; add the peeled tomatoes, the paprika and the thyme and, after cooking for at least 5 minutes, add the potato cut into small cubes and the thinly sliced cabbage.

Cook on a low heat, adding a little water; mash the cooked beans and add them, together with their cooking water. Just before removing from the heat, after cooking for about 20 minutes, add salt to taste. In the meantime, place two layers of thin slices of bread in a large earthenware bowl, then pour the soup over the bread; make two more layers of bread, and cover again with the soup.

At this point the soup is excellent. The ribollita (re-boiled) itself is prepared the next day, when the earthenware bowl is put on a low heat; a cavity is made in the centre into which is poured some extra virgin olive oil; place a wire net under the bowl to protect it from the flames and let the soup simmer very gently.

RICE WITH PORK CHOPS
◀ Lombardy ▶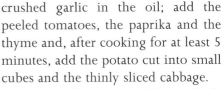

400 g of rice, 4 pork chops, butter and other fats (oil, lard, other fats of choice), 1 white onion, grated Parmesan cheese, salt, pepper.

Bring to the boil 2 litres of water (double the volume of the rice) if possible in a copper saucepan; slowly pour in the rice in order to form a cone in the saucepan with the point jutting a few millimetres out of the water. Shake the saucepan a couple of times, cover and cook on high heat for 10-12 minutes.

Remove from the heat, stir well, cover

with a thick cloth, and place the lid on top of the cloth; leave to stand for another 15 minutes.

Grate the onion and lightly brown in the butter, add salt and pepper to taste, then add the flavourings (fats) to the rice together with grated Parmesan cheese.

Serve the rice directly on the diners' plates, together with a pork chop (the puntèl, or prop, as it is called), which has previously been browned in a frying pan with a little of the flavourings (fats).

RISOTTO *ALLA PILOTA* WITH SALAMI PASTE
◀ *Veneto* ▶

400 g of rice, 4 small salamis or the equivalent quantity of fresh salami meat, 8 dl approx. of broth, grated Parmesan cheese, butter, salt.

Bring the broth to the boil on a high heat, sprinkle in the rice – it must be completely covered by the broth – shake the casserole by the handles and boil fast for 12 minutes.

Cover, remove from the heat and wrap the saucepan in a cloth, leave to stand in a warm place for 15 minutes.

In the meantime, remove the skin from the salamis and crumble the meat into a pan and brown with a knob of butter. Add this flavouring to the cooked rice – which must be dry, firm, and with the grains not sticking to each other – and add abundant grated Parmesan cheese. Mix the ingredients well and serve.

An alternative, light version is with minced lean pork instead of the salami meat. In this case, however, it is necessary to add more flavouring.

BOLETE MUSHROOM RISOTTO

◆ 📷

300 g of rice, 300 g of bolete mushrooms, 3 shallots, 1 clove of garlic, 1 bunch of parsley, broth, ¹/₂ glass of brandy, grated Parmesan cheese (optional), butter, extra virgin olive oil, salt, pepper in grains.

◆ Clean and slice the mushrooms, brown them in the oil for 10 minutes, add the finely chopped parsley and the crushed garlic, the salt and pepper, then remove from the heat.

◆ In a casserole, soften the grated shallots in oil, pour on the rice and mix together. Pour on the brandy and allow it to evaporate, always stirring.

◆ At this point add the mushrooms to the rice and, after a few moments, pour on a couple of ladlefuls of hot broth.

◆ Add salt and cook the rice, adding a ladleful of hot broth from time to time as necessary. Garnish with butter, pepper, a few spoonfuls of Parmesan cheese and a little more finely chopped parsley; remove from the heat and leave to thicken for 5 minutes.

TRUFFLE RISOTTO
◀ Piedmont ▶

400 g of rice, 1 small white truffle, 1 shallot, broth, ½ glass of dry white wine, butter, pepper in grains.

Grate the shallot and soften it in the butter; add the rice and mix well, blending the ingredients. Pour on the wine and let it evaporate; cook the rice adding as much broth as is necessary, one ladleful at a time. Brush the truffle and wash it in the white wine, then cut the outer skin and grate it finely. Remove the rice from the heat when it is still firm and flavour it with a knob of butter and the grated truffle, sprinkle over freshly ground pepper and leave it to stand for a few minutes with the lid on the saucepan. Serve garnished with a few thin slices of truffle on the top.

RICE *SARTÙ*
◀ Campania ▶

400 g of rice, 300 g of minced beef, 200 g of chicken livers, 1 Italian sausage, 250 g of fresh peas, 25 g of dried mushrooms, 60 g of grated Parmesan cheese, 1 mozzarella, 3 eggs, 1 onion, 1½ l of broth, 2-3 spoonfuls of concentrated tomato purée, white flour, bread crumbs, 200 g of lard, extra virgin olive oil, salt, pepper.

Gently fry the grated onion in an earthenware casserole, add the tomato purée diluted in a glass of broth, the mushrooms softened in warm water and squeezed and minced, the peas, salt, pepper and a piece of sausage; cook the sauce for about 20 minutes.

In the meantime mix together in a bowl the minced meat with salt and pepper, an egg, a spoonful of breadcrumbs and one of grated cheese. Make lots of little balls with this mixture, roll them in the flour and fry them in hot oil. Cook the rice in a large casserole with half of the sauce, adding a little hot broth, little by little as necessary. When the rice is cooked, remove it from the heat, and thicken it with 50 g of lard, 2 eggs and 4 spoonfuls of grated cheese. Place the remaining sauce on the heat again for a few minutes together with the meatballs and 50 g of lard.

Wash, dry and mince the chicken livers, and cook them in a little broth. Lightly butter a mould, cover the sides with rice and in the centre place the following layers: meatballs, chicken livers, pieces of mozzarella, pieces of sausage, grated cheese. Continue until the ingredients are finished. Sprinkle breadcrumbs on the top of this *sartù* and place a knob of lard here and there, then put the mould in the oven at 160°C for about half an hour. Remove from the oven and take the *sartù* out of the mould, turning it upside down on a serving plate; serve piping hot.

SCRIPELLE 'MBUSSE
◀ *Abruzzo, Molise* ▶

4 eggs, white flour, 1 sprig of parsley, ¹/₂ glass of milk, 1¹/₂ l of meat broth, 100 g of grated sheep's milk cheese, extra virgin olive oil, salt, pepper in grains.

Prepare a batter with the eggs, the finely chopped parsley, the milk, a pinch of salt and a little freshly ground pepper; add the flour, mixing it in completely. In a small lightly oiled pan pour a spoonful of the batter; the result will be a small pancake; turn over and brown on both sides. Proceed in this way until all the batter has been used. Dust the pancakes with a generous sprinkling of grated sheep's milk cheese and roll them up. Put two rolls on each plate, pour some hot meat broth, prepared in advance, over them, dust with a little more grated Parmesan cheese and serve.

SPAGHETTI WITH WILD ASPARAGUS
◀ *Umbria* ▶

400 g of spaghetti, 200 g of wild asparagus, 1 clove of garlic, 400 g of tomato pulp, extra virgin olive oil, salt, black pepper in grains.

For this recipe the asparagus that grows wild in the countryside is particularly good. Use only the tips; wash them and cook gently in a little oil with garlic. After about 10 minutes add the tomato pulp and the salt; the sauce will be ready as soon as it starts to thicken. In the meantime, bring the water for the pasta to the boil. Boil the spaghetti, drain when still firm and add the sauce, completing it with a little freshly ground black pepper.

SPAGHETTI WITH GARLIC, OIL AND PEPPER
◀ *Abruzzo, Molise* ▶

400 g of spaghetti, 4 cloves of garlic, 1 red peppercorn, 1 glass of extra virgin olive oil, salt.

Boil the pasta in abundant salted water, and in the meantime heat the oil with the broken up peppercorn in a small frying pan, then add the finely sliced garlic and leave it to brown. When the pasta is cooked but still firm, drain and add the flavoured oil. If a less spicy sauce is preferred, remove the peppercorn from the oil before adding the garlic.
If, instead, a less garlicky sauce is preferred, leave the crushed garlic cloves in the cold oil, then remove them before heating the oil and adding the peppercorn. Remember that spaghetti with this dressing must be served piping hot.

BLACK CUTTLEFISH SPAGHETTI
◀ *Veneto* ▶

400 g of spaghetti, 400 g of small cuttlefish and a few bags of their ink, 5 ripe tomatoes (optional), 1 clove of garlic, 1 bunch of parsley, extra virgin olive oil, salt, red pepper.

Clean and wash the cuttlefish, then roughly mince them. Fry the crushed garlic gently in a little oil, add the cuttlefish and a ladleful of hot water and cook for 15 minutes. Add the roughly mashed tomatoes (peeled and with the seeds removed); when the liquid of the sauce has evaporated, break the ink bags into the frying pan.

Flavour with a bunch of finely chopped parsley, salt and red pepper. Leave to absorb the flavours for a few minutes before adding the spaghetti, which in the meantime has been boiled until firm, and drained.

A variation of this recipe is without tomatoes; in this case it is possible to add a little dry white wine when cooking the cuttlefish or a few ladlefuls of hot broth.

SPAGHETTI WITH TOMATOES AND OLIVES

◀ *Puglia* ▶ 📷

400 g of spaghetti, 500 g of firm, ripe tomatoes, 150 g of black and green olives, 2 spoonfuls of pickled capers, 1 clove of garlic, marjoram or basil, paprika, extra virgin olive oil, salt.

After placing the tomatoes in boiling water for a moment, peel them, remove the seeds and mince them. In a small frying pan, cook the crushed garlic gently in a few spoonfuls of oil, then, before it browns, add the tomatoes, the green olives cut into small pieces and the whole stoned black olives, and the capers which have been rinsed under running water and dried. Add salt and cook on a moderate heat. Just before removing from the heat, add the marjoram (or the finely shopped basil), the paprika and a dribble of un-cooked oil.

Boil the spaghetti and garnish immediately after draining with the sauce and serve.

SPAGHETTI WITH RAGOUT

◀ *Abruzzo, Molise* ▶

For the spaghetti: 400 g of flour, 2 spoonfuls of lard, salt.

For the ragout: 1 slice of pork weighing 500 g, 4 slices of un-smoked bacon, 1 piece of lard, 500 g of firm, ripe tomatoes, 3 cloves of garlic, 1 sprig of parsley, red wine, 1 spoonful of lard, fresh peppercorns, salt, pepper in grains.

Knead the flour with a little lard, salt and enough water to obtain a firm, elastic dough. Work it for some time, then divide it into portions and roll it out using a special pasta machine to cut strips as wide as the space between one string and another on the guitar.

Without this particular machine, which has wires on which the pasta is laid and pressed with the rolling pin so that it is cut by the wires, use the apparatus of a normal pasta machine that is usually used for *tagliolini*. Leave the spaghetti to dry on a floured cloth and prepare the ragout.

Crush two cloves of garlic and chop finely a little parsley, and mix them with the lard and a little freshly ground pepper, then spread this paste on the slices of pork that have been lightly pounded. Place the slices of bacon on the lard, and then a few pieces of sheep's milk cheese. Wrap the meat around itself to form rolls and fix these using toothpicks or

kitchen thread. Heat the lard cut into small pieces in an earthenware saucepan with the remaining garlic clove, then place the meat in it to brown.

Pour on the wine and, as soon as it has evaporated, flavour with salt and pepper; add the roughly minced tomatoes, which have been peeled after being immersed for a moment in boiling water and from which the seeds have been removed. Cook the sauce; before removing it from the heat, take the meat and keep it hot. Boil the spaghetti in abundant salted water, drain it when it is cooked but still firm, and add the sauce. The meat, instead, will be used for the main course.

SPAGHETTI *ALLA CARBONARA*
◀ *Lazio* ▶ 🔟

400 g of spaghetti, 200 g of lean lard (from the pig's cheek) or lean un-smoked bacon, 4 eggs, 1 clove of garlic, 2 spoonfuls of grated Parmesan cheese, 1 spoonful of grated sheep's milk cheese, extra virgin olive oil, salt, pepper in grains.

Cut the lard into small cubes of about $1/2$ cm and brown them in a frying pan together with a few spoonfuls of oil and the garlic clove

(which must be removed as soon as it begins to brown).

In a hot soup bowl, mix the eggs well (two whole eggs and two yolks) at room temperature with the grated cheese, adding salt and abundant freshly ground pepper, to obtain a smooth cream.

The preparation of the dressing must be carried out when the pasta is almost ready to be drained; the pasta is put into the soup bowl, and immediately mixed with the egg and the hot crusty bacon. Serve the *carbonara* piping hot.

SPAGHETTI WITH BOTARGO
◀ *Sardinia* ▶

400 g of spaghetti, 3 slices of botargo, $1/2$ clove of garlic, $1/2$ lemon, 2 spoonfuls of extra virgin olive oil, pepper.

The botargo, which is a kind of small hard salami sausage, nut-grey in colour, is nothing other than the ovary of the grey mullet, preserved in salt. It can be sliced very thinly for the preparation of savoury tarts or grated to flavour simple white pasta. Boil the spaghetti, and in the meantime melt the botargo in a pan with the oil and a little water taken from that in which the pasta is cooked; as soon as it dissolves, dilute with the lemon juice.

Drain the pasta when it is cooked but still firm, and put it into the pan with the botargo, sprinkle with freshly ground pepper and finely chopped parsley, crushed garlic and, if desired, with a few more small pieces of botargo.

SPAGHETTI WITH PILCHARDS
◀ *Calabria* ▶

400 g of spaghetti, 300 g of fresh pilchards, 100 g of wild fennel, 30 g of pine kernels, 20 g of raisins, 4 anchovy fillets, 1 onion, extra virgin olive oil, salt, pepper.

Wash and chop finely the wild fennel. In a frying pan, brown the sliced onion in abundant oil, add the fennel, the pine kernels, the raisins (softened in warm water and then squeezed to eliminate the excess liquid) and the anchovy fillets. After a few minutes add the pilchards, which have been cleaned and de-scaled, and a little warm water, add salt and pepper and cook. Boil the spaghetti in abundant salted water, drain when they are cooked but still firm and dress with the fish sauce.

74

SPAGHETTI WITH BEST COCKLES
◀ *Lazio* ▶

400 g of spaghetti, 1 kg best cockles, 2 cloves of garlic, 1 red peppercorn, dry white wine (optional), extra virgin olive oil, salt.

Clean the cockles under running water, then leave then soaking for at least half an hour in salted water to remove any sand inside the shells. Put the cockles into a covered pan on a high heat to open the cockles, together with abundant oil, 1 sliced garlic clove, the peppercorn and, if desired, a little wine.

In the meantime, boil the spaghetti, drain it when cooked but still firm, and put it into the pan with the cockles. Mix together on a low heat and dust with crushed garlic and finely chopped parsley, then serve. Since the sauce is not filtered, it is necessary to clean the shellfish very well before cooking to avoid any unpleasant sand remaining.

STRACCIATELLA
◀ *Lazio* ▶

3 spoonful of semolina, 3 eggs, $1\frac{1}{2}$ l of meat broth, nutmeg, 50 g of grated Parmesan cheese, salt.

Bring the meat broth to the boil. In the meantime; beat the eggs, and stir in the semolina, the grated Parmesan cheese and a sprinkling of grated nutmeg. Add salt and mix well, then pour the boiling broth onto the mixture, stirring continuously cook for 5 minutes. An alternative version is without semolina.

STRANGOLAPRETI
◀ *Trentino-Alto Adige* ▶

300 g of spinach. 2 stale bread rolls, 2 eggs, 2 spoonfuls of white flour, a few sage leaves, milk, grated Parmesan cheese, butter, salt.

Strangolapreti, a typical dish of the Alto Adige region, can also be prepared with nettles, beet, or wild spinach. Clean the spinach carefully, wash and steam or boil in a little salted water, drain and squeeze it and chop finely. In the meantime, crumble the bread and dampen it with a little milk, then add the eggs, the flour and a little salt. Mix well, then stir in the spinach and from this mixture make dumplings as big as large hazelnuts.
Boil in abundant salted water until they rise to the surface (it is better to cook a few at a time, to avoid them sticking to each other), remove them with a perforated ladle. Serve with grated Parmesan cheese and melted butter flavoured with a few sage leaves.

MUSHROOM
TAGLIATELLE
◆

400 g of tagliatelle, 300 g of wild mushrooms, 3 cloves of garlic, parsley, red pepper, extra virgin olive oil, salt.

Clean the mushrooms, eliminating any inedible parts, and wash them quickly under running water, without drenching them.
Dry them carefully and slice them directly into a saucepan containing the oil and the crushed cloves of garlic. Scald briefly, then cook slowly on a low heat, add the salt and the red pepper just before they have finished cooking.
When the mushrooms are ready, boil the pasta, drain it when cooked but still firm, then put it into a large hot serving bowl, add the mushrooms and mix together, adding a dribble of raw oil and the finely chopped parsley.

TAGLIATELLE
WITH ANCHOVIES AND BREAD
◀ *Liguria* ▶

400 g of tagliatelle, 6 salted anchovies, 4 spoonfuls of grated breadcrumbs, 25 g of pine kernels, 3 cloves of garlic, parsley, red peppercorn, extra virgin olive oil, salt.

Remove the salt from the anchovies, and remove the scales with a knife and a damp cloth. Cook them in half a glassful of oil to which has been added the garlic cloves (which must be removed as soon as they begin to brown) and a few pieces of a red peppercorn. Add the finely chopped parsley and the pine kernels.
Toast the breadcrumbs evenly in a non-stick frying pan, stirring them with a wooden spoon (they must become golden but not dark). In the meantime, boil the pasta in salted water and drain when cooked but still firm.
Put the pasta in a serving bowl after having mixed with it the anchovy sauce and half of the toasted breadcrumbs.
Serve with the rest of the breadcrumbs, which the diners will sprinkle over, as is usually done with grated Parmesan cheese.

PUMPKIN *TORTELLI*
(LITTLE PUMPKIN CAKES)
◀ *Lombardy* ▶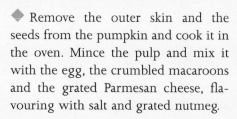

<u>For the tortelli</u>: 400 g of flour, 4 eggs, salt.
<u>For the filling</u>: 1 kg of yellow pumpkin, 100 g of almond macaroons, 150 g of grated Parmesan cheese, 1 egg, nutmeg, salt.
<u>For the dressing</u>: sage leaves, butter, grated Parmesan cheese.

◆ Remove the outer skin and the seeds from the pumpkin and cook it in the oven. Mince the pulp and mix it with the egg, the crumbled macaroons and the grated Parmesan cheese, flavouring with salt and grated nutmeg.

◆ For the pasta dough, mix the ingredients and knead until the dough has an evenly firm consistency and a shiny surface.

◆ Flour the work surface and roll out the dough very thinly with a rolling pin (and/or a pasta machine), and cut into little squares, in the middle of which place a little of the pumpkin filling.

◆ Fold the pasta squares in half, pressing down the edges to close. Boil in abundant salted water, drain and serve dressed with the melted butter and sage. Accompany with grated Parmesan cheese.

In some variations the filling is prepared with Cremona mustard (approx. 100 g) finely minced and softened in a little of its own syrup.

TAGLIATELLE
WITH BOLOGNESE RAGOUT
◀ *Emilia Romagna* ▶

<u>For the tagliatelle</u>: 400 g of flour, 4 eggs, salt.
<u>For the sauce</u>: 200 g of minced beef, 50 g of lean un-smoked bacon, $\frac{1}{2}$ onion, 1 small carrot, $\frac{1}{2}$ stick of celery, 2 spoonfuls of concentrated tomato purée, $\frac{1}{2}$ glassful of red wine, broth, grated Parmesan cheese, extra virgin olive oil, salt, pepper.

Bolognese ragout is the most traditional of all the Italian meat sauces, and it is a suitable accompaniment to the first course, *polenta* (maize porridge), etc.
To prepare the ragout, grate the onion, the carrot and the celery and separately mince the bacon. Fry the bacon lightly with a few spoonfuls of oil; when the fat has melted, mixing in the grated vegetables and, as soon as they are soft, add the minced beef.
Keep stirring so that the meat becomes uniformly brown, then pour on the wine and allow it to evaporate. Add the concentrated tomato purée diluted in a little hot broth, and the salt and pepper; lower the heat, cover the pan, and continue cooking for about 2 hours.
Add a little broth from time to time. The recipe can be varied at pleasure using different meats, adding a few chicken livers, flavouring with dried mushrooms and the water they are softened in, eliminating the tomatoes, etc.
Prepare the pasta dough and cut it into long strings 1 cm wide; leave them to dry on a floured surface. Boil the *tagliatelle*, drain them when cooked but still firm, and mix in some of the ragout. Bring to the table with the rest of the ragout in a sauceboat and with grated Parmesan cheese.

TAGLIOLINI WITH TRUFFLES
AND MUSHROOMS
◆

400 g of tagliolini, 300 g of mixed mushrooms, 100 g of black truffle, 200 g of peeled tomatoes, 1 onion, 1 clove of garlic, extra virgin olive oil, salt.

Clean the mushrooms very carefully, wash them under running water, dry them and slice them. Pour a few spoonfuls of oil into the pan and fry delicately on a low heat the finely sliced garlic and onion, add the mushrooms and leave to brown for a few minutes. Add salt to taste, then add the minced tomatoes, and cook on a moderate heat. Boil the *tagliolini* and drain them when cooked but still firm.
Put the *tagliolini* on a hot serving dish, dress with the mushroom sauce and

garnish with truffle flakes cut at the moment of serving.

POTATO *TORTELLI* (LITTLE POTATO CAKES)

◀ *Emilia Romagna* ▶

For the tortelli: 500 g of flour, 4 eggs.
For the filling: 500 g of potatoes, $1/2$ onion, 1 spoonful of tomato purée, 1 egg, 50 g of butter, 200 g of grated Parmesan cheese, salt.
For the dressing: grated Parmesan cheese, butter.

To prepare the pasta, knead all the ingredients together to make a firm dough. Flour a work surface and roll out the dough very thinly with a rolling pin. Boil the un-peeled potatoes, peel them and mash them with a potato masher.
Melt the butter in a casserole and add the finely sliced onion; when the onion begins to brown, add the tomato purée diluted in a little hot water, and add a couple of spoonfuls of water to the mixture.
Cook for a little, then remove the onion and mix the liquid into the mashed potatoes. Add the eggs, the grated Parmesan cheese and a pinch of salt. Continue stirring to make a smooth mixture. At this point, finish preparing the tortelli: from the thinly rolled out dough, cut long strips about 10 cm wide and cut them with a wheel cutter to form rectangles about 6-7 cm by 10. Place a little of the filling in the centre of each rectangle. Fold the rectangles in half with the filling in the middle.
Press the rectangles to eliminate any air that could break open the tortelli during cooking and press closed. Fill a large saucepan half full with salted water, bring to the boil and then place the tortelli into the water; boil for 10-15 minutes.
When cooked, the tortelli must be removed with a perforated ladle and well drained, taking care not to break them. Place them in layers in a serving bowl, putting melted butter and abundant grated Parmesan cheese on each layer.

TORTELLINI WITH RAGOUT

◀ *Emilia Romagna* ▶

For the tortellini: 500 g of flour, 4 eggs.
For the filling: 150 g of raw ham, 100 g of pork loin, 100 g of veal, 1 thick slice of Bologna sausage, 2 eggs, nutmeg, 100 g of grated Parmesan cheese, butter, salt, pepper.
For the sauce: meat ragout.

To make the pasta dough, mix the ingredients together and knead until the dough is firm. Flour the work surface and roll out the dough very thinly with a rolling pin (and/or a pasta machine).
Mince the meats and gently fry in a frying pan with a knob of butter, mince the ham and the Bologna sausage and then add them to the pan; blend in the egg, the Parmesan cheese, a pinch of grated nutmeg, salt and pepper. Cut the thinly rolled out dough into small 4-5 cm squares. On each square place a little of the filling, close it diagonally to form a triangle. Press the edges together well to close, and fold this around a finger, sticking the two ends together and turning up the outer corner.

Cook the tortellini in salted water or in the meat broth, drain and dress with the meat ragout, or only with melted butter flavoured with a sage leaf.

TRENETTE AL PESTO
◀ *Liguria* ▶

400 g of trenette, 30 basil leaves, 1 clove of garlic, 1-2 spoonfuls pine kernels, 1 spoonful grated sheep's milk cheese, 1 spoonful grated Parmesan cheese, extra virgin olive oil, salt.

Wash the basil leaves, dry them and squash them with a pestle and stone mortar (using a circular movement against the sides) together with the garlic and the pine kernels; after a while add the grated cheese and a pinch of salt.
As soon as the mixture is even, dilute it using the pestle in way of a spoon, with as much oil as is necessary to obtain a smooth paste that is not too fluid. The sauce can also be successfully made in a food mixer.
Boil the trenette in abundant salted water, drain and dress with the pesto diluted with two spoonfuls of the cooking water.
For this traditional recipe from Liguria, the trenette can be substituted by trofie, short pasta sticks, twisted like corkscrews.

VINCIGRASSI
◀ *The Marches* ▶

For the dough: 400 g of flour, 200 g of semolina, 5 eggs, 40 g of butter, Vinsanto, salt.
For the béchamel: 60 g of butter, 50 g of flour, 6 dl of milk, nutmeg, salt, pepper.

For the sauce: 100 g of fat ham, 1 small onion, 300 g of chicken giblets, 450 g of veal sweetbreads and tripe, white wine, 250 g of tomato pulp, 200 g of Parmesan cheese, nutmeg, broth, butter, extra virgin olive oil, salt, pepper.

Put the flour, the semolina, the eggs, the melted butter, a little salt, and a little Vinsanto in a bowl.
Knead together and leave to stand for about half an hour, then roll out the dough thinly and cut into strips 20 cm wide and about 15 cm long.
Boil them in abundant salted water, draining them when half cooked; place them on a cloth to cool. To prepare the sauce, fry the fat ham and the grated onion in oil, add the chicken giblets cut into very small pieces, and leave to cook for a few minutes; pour the white wine into the pan.
As soon as it has evaporated, add the tomato pulp, salt, pepper and a pinch of grated nutmeg; after a quarter of an hour add the sweetmeats and the tripe cut into very small pieces, add salt to taste, cover and boil for an hour and a half (if necessary adding hot broth during the cooking).
In the meantime, prepare the béchamel sauce: melt the butter on a low heat and add the flour, dilute with hot milk added little by little, stirring continuously. As soon as the sauce begins to boil cook it for 10 minutes, always stirring, and just before removing from the heat, flavour with salt, pepper and a pinch of grated nutmeg.
Butter an oven tray and place the pasta on it in layers, with a little béchamel, grated Parmesan cheese, the sauce and a few knobs of butter between each layer; continue until all the

ingredients are finished. Cover the last layer of pasta, with the béchamel and grated Parmesan cheese. Put into the oven and cook for approx. 30-40 minutes.

SICILIAN SOUP
◀ *Sicily* ▶ 📷

1 kg mixed fish suitable for soup, 1 ½ l of fish broth, 4 salted anchovy fillets, 15 stoned olives, 3 cloves of garlic, 1 bunch of basil leaves, 1 cup of raisins, 1 cup of capers, 1 cup of tomato purée, extra virgin olive oil, salt, pepper, slices of home-made type bread.

Put a generous dose of oil in an earthenware bowl and flavour with the crushed garlic cloves and heat gently; remove the garlic and add the tomato purée. Add the raisins softened in warm water, the anchovy fillets from which the salt has been washed away (taking care not to break them up), the olives and the capers, and mix well. Cook for a few minutes, then pour the hot fish broth (or water) into the bowl. Bring to the boil, and after 20 minutes add the fish that must be well covered by the liquid; add a few more ladlefuls of broth (or water) if necessary. Cover and leave to cook for

another 20 minutes; just before removing from the heat, add the finely chopped basil, then serve on slices of toasted bread.

CHICK PEA SOUP
◀ *The Marches* ▶

250 g of chick peas, 1 onion, 2 sticks of celery, 3 tomatoes, 1 carrot, a few chard leaves, 2 cloves of garlic, grated sheep's milk cheese, extra virgin olive oil, salt, bread croutons.

Slice the onions and the chard leaves, cut the celery and the carrots into very small pieces, crush the garlic, cut the tomatoes into pieces and put them all into a saucepan together with the chickpeas which have previously soaked for 24 hours and then drained. Add 1 ½ litres of water and cook for about 2 hours, add salt to taste, and add a little oil; pour the soup into individual soup bowls on top of bread croutons. Sprinkle the single helpings with sheep's milk cheese.

BROAD BEAN
AND CHICORY SOUP
◀ *Puglia* ▶

6 cups of fresh, shelled broad beans, 2 bunches of chicory, 2 onions, basil, extra virgin olive oil, salt.

Boil the broad beans in 1 ½ litres of water, drain and put aside the cooking water, mash half of the beans in a vegetable masher; wash the chicory and scald it in the water in which the beans were cooked, then chop finely. Wash and slice the onions in half moon shapes; oil the bottom of a

saucepan and heat quickly for a new minutes. Put the chicory, the mashed beans and a little of the cooking water into the saucepan, then add the whole beans; bring to the boil and remove from the heat. Add a little un-cooked oil at the moment of serving and garnish with basil leaves.

MAIZE SOUP
◀ *Friuli Venezia-Giulia* ▶

250 g of dried beans, 250 g of maize, 1 carrot, 1 onion, 1 stick of celery, 50 g of lard, salt, pepper in grains.

Soak the beans overnight in warm water, then drain and boil together with the maize grains for a couple of hours; add salt towards the end of the cooking. Gently fry the grated carrot, onion and celery in the lard and add to the soup; leave to cook for a few more minutes then remove from the heat. Serve the soup piping hot, adding a generous dose of freshly ground pepper at the moment of serving.

CELERY SOUP
◀ *Calabria* ▶

600 g of celery, 200 g of Italian sausage, 200 g of Caciocavallo cheese, 3 eggs, grated sheep's milk cheese, extra virgin olive oil, salt, pepper, homemade type bread.

Wash the celery and cut it into pieces, and place them in a saucepan with 1½ litres of water, a few spoonfuls of oil, salt and pepper.
Simmer until the celery is softened. Crumble the sausage, cut the Caciocavallo cheese into small cubes, hard boil the eggs, remove the shells and cut them into segments.
Place all these ingredients on toasted slices of bread arranged in a serving bowl, pour on the celery soup, garnish with grated sheep's milk cheese and serve piping hot.

SOUP WITH FRIED OFFAL
◀ *Campania* ▶

1 kg all together of pig's heart, spleen and lungs, 1½ l of meat broth, 1 glass of red wine, rosemary, tomato purée, 30 g of lard, extra virgin olive oil, salt, red peppercorn, pepper, bread croutons.

Leave the pig offal under running water for about one hour. Heat equal quantities of oil and lard in a frying pan; add the offal cut into small pieces and leave to fry gently.
Pour over the red wine and allow to evaporate. Cover with tomato purée, flavour with salt, pepper, red peppercorn and rosemary. Add the boiling hot meat broth, ladle by ladle, and cook on a low heat for about an hour.
Serve the soup steaming hot accompanied by bread croutons.

MAIN
MEAT
COURSES

ROAST SPRING LAMB WITH POTATOES
◀ *Lazio* ▶

1 kg or more of leg and shoulder of spring lamb (very young lamb), 70 g of fat and lean ham, 1 kg potatoes, garlic, rosemary, bay leaves, 1/₂ glass of dry white wine, lard, extra virgin olive oil, salt, pepper.

Prick the meat of the lamb with a long, thin bladed knife and insert into the cuts a few garlic cloves, small rosemary sprigs and pieces of fat and lean ham; grease the lamb with the lard and sprinkle with salt and pepper.
Put it on an oven tray with oil and a few bay leaves; around the meat arrange the peeled potatoes, sprinkling them with salt and pepper, and a dribble of oil. Put into the oven and, after about half an hour, pour the white wine over the lamb.
During cooking, turn the potatoes and the roast over now and then to avoid them sticking to the tray. Cook for another 30 minutes and, when the lamb and the potatoes are nice and brown, remove from the oven, cut the meat and serve.

ROAST CHINE OF PORK
◆ 🔲

1 kg pork loin, 1 sprig of rosemary, 2 cloves of garlic, 1 clove, broth, extra virgin olive oil, salt, black pepper.

Crush the garlic and crumble the rosemary, and salt and pepper the meat, then pour oil over it and arrange the garlic and the rosemary and the clove on it. Tie it with kitchen thread and put it into a medium hot oven.

Cook the chine for about 2 hours, turning it over frequently to brown it uniformly and adding a ladleful of hot broth if it becomes too dry: the meat inside must remain white and tender.
It can be served thinly sliced either hot or cold.

FLORENTINE STEAKS
◀ *Tuscany* ▶

1 veal Florentine steak weighing about 600 g for every 2 diners, extra virgin olive oil, salt, pepper.

For the famous Florentine steak it is essential to use the meat of young oxen; the chop must be cut to include both fillet and sirloin and must be about 2 cm thick.
Put the steaks on the grill, if possible over an open wood fire, and cook them for 5-6 minutes each side, then flavour them with salt and pepper; leave a moment longer over the fire and then serve immediately, dressed with a dribble of raw extra virgin olive oil.

MIXED BOILED MEATS
◀ *The Aosta Valley, Piedmont* ▶ 🔲

1 kg of beef, 1 farm-yard chicken, 500 g of calf's head, 500 g of tongue in salamoia, 1 Italian pork sausage, 2 onions, 2 carrots, 1 stick of celery, salt.

Put the chicken and the beef together in a large saucepan; add water and salt and simmer for 2 hours, removing the froth every now and then.

Separately cook the sausage, the calf's head and the tongue. Serve the meats piping hot and sliced.

Traditionally, boiled meats are brought to the table accompanied by the following recommended sauces.

Red sauce

4 large, very ripe tomatoes, $^{1}/_{2}$ sweet pepper, $^{1}/_{2}$ stick of celery, 1 onion, 1 clove of garlic, 1 sprig of basil, 1 sprig of parsley, 1 sprig of rosemary, 1 red peppercorn, extra virgin olive oil, salt.

Peel the tomatoes and cook gently in the oil with the vegetables, the flavourings and a pinch of salt. When cooked, mince with the vegetable mincer and bring back to the boil.

Remove from the heat and dribble a little un-cooked olive oil over it.

Green sauce

1 sprig of rosemary, 2 eggs, 2 anchovy fillets, 8 capers, bread without the crust, 1 clove of garlic, vinegar, extra virgin olive oil, salt.

Mince together the parsley, the garlic, the yolks of the eggs, already hard-boiled, the anchovy fillets, the capers, and a little bread soaked in vinegar. Mix together the various ingredients, adding salt and enough oil to make a smooth, even sauce.

BRAISED BEEF WITH BAROLO

◀ *The Aosta Valley, Piedmont* ▶

$1^{1}/_{2}$ kg of beef, 1 piece of fat raw ham, 2 onions, 2 carrots, 1 stick of celery, 1 bay leaf, 2-3 sage leaves, 1 sprig of rosemary, 3 glasses of Barolo wine, extra virgin olive oil, salt, pepper.

Gently fry the beef in the oil with the fat ham cut into small cubes, pour over the wine and lower the heat.

Add the flavourings: the onion, the carrots, the stick of celery, all cut into small pieces, the bay, sage and rosemary leaves. Add salt, pepper, and a few glasses of water and cook slowly for about 2 hours.

Cut the meat into slices and serve it with the sauce produced during the cooking and which has been passed through the vegetable masher.

BAKED KID
◀ *Sardinia* ▶

2 pieces of kid (shoulder and back), 2 cloves of garlic, 1 sprig of rosemary, a few basil leaves, a few myrtle leaves, 2 slices of lard, 1 spoonful of bread crumbs, extra virgin olive oil, salt, pepper.

Salt and pepper the pieces of kid, wrap them in the slices of lard, grease the baking tray with a little oil, place the kid on it and cook in a moderate oven. Every now and then turn the pieces of meat over and pour some of the cooking sauce over them.

In the meantime, peel the garlic, wash and dry the parsley, the basil

and the myrtle, chop them all finely and mix with the breadcrumbs.

Remove the baking tray from the oven, put the pieces of meat on a bed of herbs and breadcrumbs and put it back in the oven for a few minutes, raising the heat so that the meat will brown. Serve very hot.

STEWED VENISON
◀ *Trentino-Alto Adige* ▶

1 kg of venison, 50 g of un-smoked bacon, 5-6 bay leaves, red wine, broth, butter, extra virgin olive oil, salt, pepper.
<u>For the marinade</u>: *1 litre of red wine, 5-6 sage leaves, 2-3 sprigs of rosemary, thyme, 3-4 cloves.*

Leave the venison to marinate for 24 hours immersed in red wine flavoured with the sage leaves, the rosemary, the clove and a few sprigs of thyme. After this period, heat the bacon together with a little oil and a piece of butter in a casserole, remove the meat from the marinade, drain and cut into pieces and brown in the casserole with the bacon.

Add salt and pepper to taste, pour a little red wine into the casserole and a little later a ladleful of broth and the bay leaves.

Cook slowly for about 2 hours, adding more broth, if necessary.

RAW MEAT
WITH ROCKET AND LEMON
◆

600 g of fillet in very thin slices, 200 g of rocket, 100 g of flakes of Parmesan cheese, 2 lemons, extra virgin olive oil, salt, pepper in grains.

Arrange the meat on a serving plate, cover with a sauce prepared by mixing together the oil and the lemon juice; add salt and freshly ground pepper at the moment of serving.

Choose young, tender rocket leaves, wash carefully, dry and arrange them uniformly on the meat.

Cover all with flakes of Parmesan cheese and serve.

CIBREO
◀ Tuscany ▶ 📷

200 g of cock crests and wattles, 100 g of chicken livers, 2 eggs, $1/2$ lemon, 1 onion, 2 sage leaves, $1/2$ l of broth, 40 g of butter, salt.

Cibreo is a traditional main course, the principal ingredient of which is composed of chicken wattles.

It can also be prepared with a side serving of vegetables, like courgettes, carrots and French beans, which for this version of the recipe should be prepared in quantities of 50 g for each kind of vegetable.

Clean and boil the crests and wattles, cooking them for half an hour before peeling them. In the meantime, grate the onion and heat it with the butter in a large frying pan, together with the sage.

When it is golden brown, add the crests and wattles, and add a little hot broth to flavour them.

The vegetables cut into small pieces can be added. Cook on a low heat for about 20 minutes before adding the well cleaned chicken livers cut into small pieces.

In the meantime, separate the yolks of the eggs and mix them with the

lemon juice. After 10 minutes, remove from the heat and pour the yolk mixture onto the meat, stirring fast to prevent them solidifying.

Add salt to taste and put back on the heat for 2 minutes without bringing to the boil.

STEWED WILD BOAR
◀ Sardinia ▶

1 kg wild boar meat, 100 g of very thinly sliced raw ham, 1 onion, celery, parsley, vinegar, 1 glass of white wine, broth, butter, salt, pepper.

Soak the boar in the vinegar for at least half an hour, remove it, drain and cover it with the thin slices of ham, tying them with string.

Put some butter in a pan and brown the meat; add salt and pepper and continue cooking, turning the meat over every now and then.

Add the celery and the onion cut into pieces, a sprig of parsley, the white wine and the broth.

Leave to cook on a low heat for about an hour, then increase the heat to reduce the liquid before bringing to the table.

OX TAIL
ALLA VACCINARA
◀ Lazio ▶

1 kg of ox tail, 1 piece of ox cheek, 200 g of ripe, firm tomatoes, 1 onion, 1 carrot, 1 stick of celery, 1 clove of garlic, 1 handful of pine kernels, 50 g of lard, $1/2$ glass of red wine, $1/2$ glass of extra virgin olive oil, salt, pepper.

Fry gently the lard, onion, carrot, garlic and a little parsley in a casserole, add the ox tail and cheek, washed and cut into pieces, add salt and pepper and pour on the wine.

Let the meat brown evenly, then add the tomatoes, previously skinned, deseeded and mashed.

Cover the casserole and continue cooking on a very low heat for 4-5 hours, adding a ladle of hot salted water if it becomes too dry.

When the meat is tender enough to come away from the bone, add the cleaned celery cut into pieces as long as a finger, and the pine kernels.

Cook for 20 minutes more, then serve piping hot.

An older version of this recipe includes the addition of a little plain cocoa powder.

CONIGLIO ALLA CACCIATORA (STEWED RABBIT)
◀ *The Aosta Valley* ▶

1 rabbit, 2 onions, 1 large red tomato, 2 cloves of garlic, 1 sprig of rosemary, $^1/_2$ l of white wine vinegar, dry white wine, extra virgin olive oil, salt.

Cut the rabbit into pieces which are not too small and leave them in water and vinegar for about an hour.

Drain well and dry with a cloth, and put them into a baking dish with the oil and the garlic cloves. Brown the meat evenly on all sides until it is golden brown and pour on the white wine.

Let the wine evaporate, then remove the pieces of rabbit from the dish and add the grated onion and rosemary.

When the onion is golden brown, replace the rabbit in the dish, add salt, and the tomato cut into thick slices. Then add gradually a little wine and water and cook on a moderate heat.

This dish can be served with piping hot polenta (maize porridge) and a side dish of raw seasonal vegetables.

FRIED LAMB CUTLETS

◆

8 lamb cutlets, 2 eggs, breadcrumbs, olive oil, salt.

Pound the cutlets well and place them in the lightly salted beaten egg, then in the breadcrumbs.
Put them in boiling oil, turning them frequently to brown perfectly.
When cooked, drain well, add salt and serve the cutlets very hot.

ITALIAN PORK SAUSAGE WITH SAVOY CABBAGE
◀ *Emilia Romagna* ▶

1 Italian pork sausage weighing 800 g, 1 kg of Savoy cabbage, 1 large onion, 1/2 glass of vinegar, 1 spoonful of concentrated tomato purée, 100 g of lard, 2 spoonfuls of extra virgin olive oil.

Before cooking the sausage, prick it with a fork or a toothpick and wrap it in a white cloth, tied at the ends with string that also goes from one end of the sausage to the other.
Fill a saucepan with cold water, place the sausage in the water, bring to the boil, lower the heat and cook for about 3 hours.

In the meantime, peel and grate the onion, wash the Savoy cabbage and slice it thinly, brown the onion in a large pan with the butter, the oil and the minced lard.
As soon as the onion is browned, dilute the concentrated tomato purée in a glass of hot water and pour it into the pan, add the vinegar and the thinly sliced cabbage, then simmer for about an hour, until the cabbage has absorbed the sauce well.
When the sausage is cooked, remove it from the water immediately and let it cool.
When it is quite cold, it will be possible to slice it without breaking it. Put the sausage slices back into the cabbage sauce, mix gently over a low heat, being careful not to break up the slices.

BOLOGNESE STEAKS
◀ *Emilia Romagna* ▶

4 veal rump steaks, 4 slices of raw ham, 1 egg, tomato purée, breadcrumbs, Parmesan cheese, butter, salt.

Flatten the veal steaks lightly with the meat pounder, put them into the beaten egg with a pinch of salt, then cover them with breadcrumbs.
Melt the butter in a frying pan, place the steaks in the pan and, after quickly browning them on both sides, place a slice of raw ham, some flakes of Parmesan cheese and a little tomato purée on each of them.
Cover the pan and lower the heat to a minimum. They will be ready when the cheese has melted.

PHEASANT WITH MUSH-ROOMS AND ONIONS

◀ *The Aosta Valley, Piedmont* ▶

1 pheasant, 200 g of fresh mushrooms, 12 small flat white onions, 100 g of un-smoked bacon, $\frac{1}{2}$ glass of cognac, broth, 100 g of butter, salt, pepper, bread croutons.

Pluck and clean the pheasant, cut into four parts and wrap the bacon around them. Brown the meat in a pan with the butter, turning the pieces over to colour evenly.
Add the cognac and, when it has evaporated, add a ladleful of broth.
Continue cooking, adding salt and pepper to taste and, if necessary, more broth.
Boil the onions, removing them from the heat when they are still firm; clean and slice the mushrooms and add the onions and the mushrooms to the pheasant 20 minutes before removing from heat.
Serve with bread croutons.

FALSOMAGRO

◀ *Sicily* ▶

1 slice of beef of approx. 800 g, 150 g of lean minced pork, 2 sausages, 3 slices of un-smoked of fresh sheep's milk cheese, red wine, broth, extra virgin olive oil, salt, pepper.

Boil the eggs for 8 minutes, then remove the shells. Prepare the filling for the roast mixing together the minced meat and the skinned sausage. Fry the meats gently for 10 minutes in a little oil, adding half of a sliced onion. Carefully lay the browned minced meat, the slices of bacon, the eggs in slices, the cheese in flakes and the crushed garlic on the slice of beef.

Add a little salt and pepper, then roll up the slice with all the other ingredients inside, and tie with string. Put some oil and the rest of the sliced onion into a casserole, brown the stuffed meat, add the red wine and let the wine evaporate.

Lower the heat and continue cooking; towards the end of the cooking (about 1 hour) add the broth little by little.

VENETIAN STYLE LIVER
◀ *Veneto* ▶

700 g of veal liver, 700 g of white onions, milk or vinegar, parsley, butter, extra virgin olive oil, salt.

Cut the liver into strips and leave to marinate in the milk (or water and vinegar) for at least an hour.

Slice the onions thinly and fry gently in butter and oil. Remove the liver from the marinade, drain and add to the onions; cook on a high heat. Add salt at the end of the cooking, sprinkle with finely chopped parsley and serve.

FILLET STEAK
WITH GREEN PEPPER
◆

4 slices of fillet 2½ cm thick, 3 spoonfuls of green pepper in grains, 1 clove of garlic, 4 spoonfuls of sweet mustard, 4 spoonfuls of single cream, ½ glass of extra virgin olive oil, salt.

The day before cooking the fillet, leave it in the oil with the slightly squashed pepper grains. A couple of hours

before cooking, filter out the pepper from the oil and use this to marinate the slices of meat, which have been rubbed with a clove of garlic.

In the meantime, prepare the sauce: mix well a spoonful of green pepper and a little oil with the mustard and the lightly whipped cream.

Just before serving, remove the fillet from the marinade, drain well, and cook the fillet (the time depends on the degree of cooking preferred), add salt and place on a hot plate, adding the sauce and garnishing with the remaining grains of green pepper.

FINANZIERA
◀ *The Aosta Valley, Piedmont* ▶

100 g of minced meat, 100 g of veal fillet, 100 g of tripe, 100 g of brains, 100 g of sweetbreads, 50 g of chicken livers, 50 g of pork liver, 50 g of cock crests, 50 g of kidney, 50 g of shelled peas, 100 g of bolete mushrooms in oil, 60 g of butter, 1 glassful of Barolo wine, 1 cup of broth, 1 spoonful of vinegar, 2 spoonfuls of Marsala wine, flour, salt, pepper.

Cut the fillet into strips and the kidney into pieces and brown them in the butter, adding a little broth and a pinch of salt and pepper.

Separately, prepare balls of minced meat and cut the tripe into small pieces about 3 cm big, cut into pieces the brains, the liver, the sweetbreads, the chicken livers, the pork liver and the cock crests, cover all of these with flour and brown delicately in the butter, adding lastly the shelled peas and the mushrooms sliced thinly.

When cooked, put the two mixtures together, pour the Barolo wine over

94

and simmer until the liquid is reduced. Just before serving sprinkle with the vinegar and the Marsala wine, mix well and bring to the table on an elegant serving plate.

FONDUE

◀ *The Aosta Valley, Piedmont* ▶

300 g of Fontina cheese, 4 eggs, milk, 50 g of butter, salt, pepper in grains, bread croutons.

Cut the Fontina cheese into small cubes and place them in a bowl, cover with milk and leave to stand for one night. The next day, melt the butter, the Fontina cheese and a little of the milk with the bain-marie method, stirring continuously until the cheese has completely melted.
Remove from the heat and add, one at a time, the egg yolks, a little salt and a generous dose of freshly ground pepper. Reheat, always with the bain-marie method, stirring continuously, without bringing to the boil.
When it has become a thick even cream, remove from the heat and serve the fondue in hot bowls accompanied by the bread croutons lightly toasted in the oven.

PIEDMONTESE MIXED FRY

◀ *The Aosta Valley, Piedmont* ▶

300 g of sausage, 300 g of liver, 300 g of lungs, 300 g of veal fillet, 100 g of brains, 2apples, 6 carrots, 3 potatoes, 6 almond macaroons, 200 g of semolina, ¹/₂ l of milk, 100 g of sugar, the grated rind of 1 lemon, 2 eggs, breadcrumbs, flour, olive oil, salt.

Prepare the ingredients for the mixed fry. On a low heat, mix the semolina with the milk, the sugar and the lemon rind, stirring well until the batter is like a thick cream; turn it out onto a marble work surface and, when it has cooled, cut it into diamond shapes. Cut the sausage into pieces and brown in a little oil. Clean the brains, liver and lungs and cut into strips.
Peel the apples and slice them. Cut the carrots into strips. Peel the potatoes and cut them into discs.
When the ingredients are ready, including the macaroons, cover them with a little flour, then with the beaten egg, and then with the breadcrumbs, then fry them in hot oil. Drain them on kitchen paper, sprinkle them with salt and serve piping hot.

GOULASH

◀ *Friuli Venezia-Giulia* ▶

800 g of ox muscle, 2 large onions, 2 cloves of garlic, 2 spoonful of paprika, 1 bay leaf, 1 spoonful of cumin seeds, ¹/₂ spoonful of marjoram leaves, 1 lemon, 1 glassful of red wine, 1 glassful of wine vinegar, 4 spoonfuls of lard, 1 spoonful of butter, salt.

Heat the lard in a thick bottomed saucepan, add the onions sliced into thin rings and lightly brown them; collect the rings together in a pile to one side on the bottom of the pan and, in the remaining space, brown the meat cut into smallish cubes. Mix the meat with the onions and continue to cook, until a golden crust forms on the bottom of the pan. Pour in the wine and the vinegar, allow the liquid

together, salt and pepper. Lay another slice of meat on top of each. Roll the slices up and cover with flour, then with the beaten white of the egg.

Heat a generous amount of oil and, when it is very hot, place the meat rolls in it for a few minutes. Remove and drain well on absorbent paper, and serve immediately.

LEPRE ALLA CACCIATORA (STEWED HARE)
◀ Umbria ▶

1 hare, 50 g of fat and lean ham, 1 onion, 2 anchovies, rosemary, capers, $\frac{1}{2}$ glassful of white wine, vinegar, extra virgin olive oil, salt, pepper, red peppercorn.

Clean the hare, cut it in pieces and wash it with vinegar; place it in a non-stick pan and let it dry out on a low heat, with no other ingredients. In a casserole, pour a little oil and lightly fry the onion and the ham, both minced, add the pieces of hare, flavoured with salt and pepper. While the meat is browning, prepare a mixture by mincing together the cleaned and de-boned anchovies, the rosemary and 2 spoonfuls of capers. Add this mixture to the saucepan, diluting it with a little oil and the white wine, and flavouring it with a pinch of dried peppercorn. When the wine has evaporated, cover the pan and cook slowly for about 2 hours.

to evaporate a little, add salt and a pinch of paprika, and a glass of water; leave to simmer on a moderate heat for an hour ad a half. Mince the herbs finely, mix them with the softened butter, and add to the goulash together with the rind and juice of the lemon. Before serving, leave on the heat for the flavours to blend for a few minutes.

MUSHROOM ROULADE
◆

16 very thin slices of beef round, 8 button mushrooms, 1 egg, garlic, parsley, flour, oil for frying, salt, pepper.

For the success of this dish the slices of beef round must be extremely thin. Lay out half of the slices of meat and put into the centre of each one a raw mushroom cut into very thin slices, a pinch of parsley and garlic, minced

SWEET AND SOUR HARE
◀ Friuli Venezia-Giulia ▶

1 hare, 100 g of un-smoked bacon, 1 onion, 2 carrots, 400 g of tomatoes, $\frac{1}{2}$ lemon, 1 spoonful of sugar, cinnamon, 1 handful of pine kernels,

raisins, yellow corn flour, $\frac{1}{2}$ glassful of red wine, broth, extra virgin olive oil, salt, pepper.

Clean the hare, cut it in pieces and brown it in a little oil with the bacon cut into small cubes, the grated onion and carrots. When it is golden brown, sprinkle with a generous handful of corn flour and stir in. Pour in the red wine and, as soon as it has evaporated, add the sugar, the tomatoes cut into small pieces, the cinnamon, the pine kernels and a few raisins (softened in warm water for 15 minutes and then squeezed), the grated rind of the lemon, salt and pepper. Leave for all the flavours to blend in, then add the broth and continue cooking very gently on a very low heat. Serve accompanied by hot *polenta* (maize porridge).

JUGGED HARE

◀ *The Aosta Valley; Lombardy* ▶

1 hare and its liver, 1 onion, 1 carrot, 1 stick of celery, 1 clove of garlic, 1 pear, 1 lemon, 4 walnuts, 1 spoonful of juniper berries, 2 cloves,

1 sprig of rosemary, sage, 1 of red wine, 50 g of butter, 50 g of lard, salt, pepper in grains.

Clean the hare, cut it in pieces and leave it to marinate for 2-3 days with a little wine together with the sliced celery, carrot and onion, the crushed garlic, the sliced pear, the walnuts, the juniper berries, the cloves, a few grains of pepper, the lemon rind, the sage, the rosemary and salt. After the marinating period, melt the butter in a pan together with the lard and brown the pieces of meat, removed from the marinade and drained. When they are browned sufficiently, add the vegetables and, little by little, the wine used for the marinade, continuing the cooking.

When the vegetables are cooked, remove them from the pan, mash them and replace them in the pan with the meat.

At this point, mince the liver and put it in the pan. Add more wine during cooking if necessary, add salt to taste before removing from the heat. Serve with buckwheat *polenta*.

Milanese *ossibuchi*
◀ *Lombardy* ▶

4 calf ossibuchi (vertebrae), 1 small onion, white flour, 1 lemon, parsley, 1 garlic clove, 1 salted anchovy, dry white wine, broth or water, 150 g of butter, salt, pepper.

Thoroughly flour the ossibuchi and brown in the butter, add salt and pepper and pour a little dry white wine into the pan. When the wine has evaporated, add enough hot broth (or water) for the cooking, which will take about an hour.

About ten minutes before removing from the heat add the parsley, lemon rind (only the yellow part), garlic, onion and the cleaned and washed anchovy, all minced together. Serve with a good saffron risotto.

Pesticide de cavàl (Horse meat hash)
◀ *Veneto* ▶

1 kg of foal meat, 1 kg of onions, 1 l approx. of dry red wine, 3 carrots, 2 bay leaves, 4 cloves, paprika, 1 knob of butter, extra virgin olive oil, salt, pepper.

This typical dish is a very tasty overcooked horsemeat stew, which becomes better and better the longer it is cooked.
Mince all the vegetables and brown them in a pan with the oil and butter, then add the meat cut into pieces and leave it to brown for a few minutes; add the wine, the spices, the salt and the pepper and continue cooking on a very low heat. It will be ready when the meat tends to fall apart and the

vegetables have become a purée. Serve with a good, hot polenta (maize porridge) that is not too dry.

Chicken breasts with truffles

4 chicken breasts, 1 medium sized black truffle, 80 g of raw ham, 80 g of Fontina cheese, 1 small onion, flour, broth, 1 glassful of dry sherry, 30 g of butter, extra virgin olive oil, salt.

With a sharp knife, cut into the chicken breasts horizontally to form a pocket, flatten them with the meat pounder, sprinkle them with salt and flour them lightly. Inside each pocket place two slices of ham cut to size, a slice of Fontina cheese and a slice of truffle.
Close each pocket and sew them with string or close the edges with a wooden skewer. Heat the butter and 2 spoonfuls of oil in a pan and put in it the grated onion to soften.
When it begins to soften, lay the chicken breasts in the pan and brown them on both sides. Pour on the sherry, let it evaporate and continue to cook, adding a little broth to the sauce.

Serve the stuffed breasts with a salad of seasonal vegetables or with a side dish made with truffles.

JUGGED PIGEONS
◀ *Umbria* ▶

2 pigeons, 1 onion, 1 carrot, 1 stick of celery, 1 clove of garlic, parsley, sage, rosemary, bay, 1 anchovy, white wine, vinegar, extra virgin olive oil, salt, pepper, bread croutons.

Clean the pigeons, cut them into pieces and put them into a frying pan to brown together with the onion, carrot, celery and parsley and a little oil. Add a few sage and bay leaves, the crushed rosemary, a couple of centimetres of white wine and the same quantity of vinegar. Add salt and pepper, and leave to cook for an hour.
Remove the pigeons from the pan and filter the cooking liquid. Add the cleaned and boned anchovy, the crushed garlic and a little vinegar to the liquid. Replace the pigeons in the pan with the sauce and leave them for a few minutes to absorb all the flavours on a moderate heat. Serve with fried croutons.

STUFFED PIGEONS
◀ *Basilicata* ▶

2 pigeons, 2 large slices of raw ham, not too thin, 1/2 glassful of white wine, 1 spoonful of lard.
<u>For the filling</u>: *the pigeon giblets, 1 egg, 1 clove of garlic, rosemary, 2-3 spoonfuls of bread-crumbs, extra virgin olive oil, salt, pepper.*

Pluck and clean the pigeons, keeping aside the giblets, sprinkle with salt

and pepper. Cut the giblets into small pieces and heat them, adding the breadcrumbs, a little rosemary and grated garlic, a dribble of oil, the egg yolk, and mix well together. Add a little salt. Take off the heat and leave to cool. Fill the pigeons with this mixture, sewing up the opening; wrap them up with rashers of raw ham.
Melt the lard in an oven pan, then put the pigeons on the tray and brown them evenly. Pour on the white wine and, after a few minutes, put them into the oven to cook.
Turn them over from time to time and, if necessary, add a little hot salted water; leave them to cook for 30 to 45 minutes.

POLENTA HASH
◀ *Friuli Venezia-Giulia* ▶

200 g of fine corn flour, 50 g of coarse corn flour, 200 g of heifer, 1/2 chicken, 300 g of sliced pork, 1 pigeon, 2 sausages, 1 onion, 1 carrot, thyme, sage, rosemary, 1 glassful of red wine, broth, milk, 2 spoonfuls of flour, vinegar, butter, extra virgin olive oil, salt.

A few days in advance, marinate the heifer meat in water and vinegar in a cool place. After marinating, wash it and brown it in a pan in oil and butter, together with the chopped onion, carrot, thyme, sage and rosemary. Then add the other meats, pour over the red wine, let the wine evaporate and add a glassful of broth; cook gently for about an hour.

In the meantime, prepare a soft *polenta* (maize porridge) with the fine and coarse corn flours, cooking them in water and milk. As soon as it is ready pour it out on to a carving board, leave it to cool, and when cold, cut it into slices.

Grease a baking tray with oil, arrange the slices of *polenta* in rows and cover them with the cooked, boned meats cut into pieces.

Separately, melt 2 spoonfuls of butter, add the flour and toast it. Filter the sauce produced during the cooking of the meat and use it to dilute the flour and butter mixture so that it has a creamy consistency; pour this onto the meat and the *polenta*. Put into the oven for 10 minutes, then serve.

POLENTA TARAGNA
◀ *Lombardy* ▶

400 g of buckwheat flour, 50 g of butter, 300 g of soft paste cheese (Fontina or Taleggio or, even better, Bitto), salt.

First prepare the *polenta* with the buckwheat flour (or, if preferred, buckwheat and maize flour). When it is cooked, remove the *polenta* from the heat, add the butter and the cheese cut into thin slices and put it on the heat

again for a few minutes, stirring continuously. When all the ingredients are well mixed, serve immediately, piping hot and steaming. An alternative version suggests flavouring the *Taragna polenta* with a truffle grated on top when served.

POLLO ALLA DIAVOLA (PEPPERY CHICKEN)

1 large chicken, a few slices of raw ham, 1 large slice of un-smoked bacon rosemary, 1 glassful of white wine, broth, extra virgin olive oil, salt, pepper.

Clean the chicken, removing the giblets, the head and the feet, and wash it well under running water, then dry it. Cut the bacon into pieces and place it inside the chicken, flavouring with salt and pepper. Salt the chicken inside and out, and put it into a large pan to brown with some oil and a sprig of rosemary.

Cover the pan, turn the chicken over from time to time, and add a little broth if it begins to stick to the bottom. When the chicken is cooked, cover it with the slices of raw ham and pour over the wine, leaving this to evaporate. Sprinkle with pepper and serve.

SALTIMBOCCA ALLA ROMANA
◀ *Lazio* ▶

12 small slices of veal, 200 g of raw ham, sage, dry white wine, extra virgin olive oil, salt, pepper.

Salt and pepper the slices of meat, place on each one a slice of raw ham and a sage leaf, roll each one up and fix with a toothpick. Arrange the *saltimbocca* in a frying pan with oil and cook them for a few minutes, pouring a little white wine over them. Serve with the liquid remaining from the cooking.

LEMON ESCALOPES

◆

400 g of veal slices, 2 lemons, parsley, extra virgin olive oil, salt, pepper.

Mix the juice of the lemon with a spoonful of oil and a little pepper in a soup plate, beat the slices lightly with a meat pounder and leave them to marinate in this liquid for at least 30 minutes, turning them over every now and then.
Heat a large frying pan with a few spoonfuls of oil and brown the veal on both sides, then place them on a hot serving plate.
Put the pan back on the heat and add the marinade to any liquid remaining from the cooking, and with any left-over lemon juice.
Mix and heat this sauce then pour it over the escalopes and serve sprinkled with finely chopped parsley and the grated yellow part of the lemon rind.

STEWED BEEF
◀ *Tuscany* ▶

800 g of beef, 3 cloves of garlic, rosemary, tomato pulp, ½ glass of red wine, broth (optional), extra virgin olive oil, salt, pepper, slices of home-made type bread.

Gently fry the garlic cloves in oil in a casserole until they are soft, remove them, lay the meat flavoured with the rosemary, salt and pepper, in the casserole.
Brown for a few minutes, then pour over the red wine and allow to evaporate; then add a little tomato pulp. Cover the pan and cook slowly for a couple of hours, adding, if necessary, some hot broth; during the cooking turn the meat over frequently.
Lay some slices of toasted home-made type bread on a serving plate, slice the meat and lay the slices on the bread and bring to the table.

TRIPE
◀ *Tuscany* ▶

1½ kg veal tripe, 300 g of skinned tomatoes, 100 g of un-smoked bacon, 1 stick of celery, 1 onion, 1 carrot, bay leaves, 1 glass of white wine, broth, 50 g of butter, extra virgin olive oil, salt, pepper.

Wash the tripe thoroughly under running water and then boil it in salted water for about half an hour. Apart, begin to fry the finely chopped or minced celery, onion, carrot, bacon and a few bay leaves. Add the butter, the wine, the tomatoes, salt and

pepper. Drain the tripe, and when this begins to thicken add it to the sauce; mix the ingredients well and continue cooking on a moderate heat until the tripe is really tender.

During cooking, add some hot broth from time to time, so that the food does not stick to the pan.

VEAL FRICASSÉE

◆

800 g of small pieces of veal breast, 1 onion, 1 clove of garlic, parsley or basil, 2 eggs, 1 lemon, flour, white wine, butter, extra virgin olive oil, salt.

In a casserole soften the garlic and the sliced onion with the butter and oil. Remove the garlic, cover the pieces of veal with flour and put them in the casserole.

Brown them on a high heat, pour over the white wine and allow this to evaporate. Add salt and two or three glasses of hot water, then leave to cook on a low heat until the meat is tender. If the sauce dries up, add more hot water or hot broth.

Beat two egg yolks with the lemon juice, remove the casserole from the heat and slowly stir the meat sauce until it becomes creamy.

Finally, if desired, add the finely chopped parsley or basil. Serve this meat piping hot.

VEAL WITH TUNA SAUCE
◀ *The Aosta Valley, Piedmont* ▶

1 kg of lean veal, 1 carrot, 1 onion, 1 stick of celery, 1 bay leaf, 200 g of tuna fish in olive oil, 4 anchovies, 2-3 spoonfuls capers, 2 hard boiled eggs, 1 lemon, 1 spoonful of vinegar, extra virgin olive oil, salt.

Boil the veal in salted water together with the carrot, celery, bay leaf and vinegar.

Cook it for about one and a half hours; when the meat is cooked, leave it to cool in the broth remaining from the cooking; then drain well and slice thinly.

In the meantime, mince finely (if possible with a food mixer) the tuna fish, the anchovies, the capers and the yolks of the hard boiled eggs; blend these ingredients well with oil, the juice of the lemon and, if necessary, a little of the broth. Arrange the slices on an elegant serving plate and cover completely with the sauce.

Leave to stand for a couple of hours in a cool place, then serve.

MAIN
FISH
COURSES

SWORD FISH *ACCHIOTTA*
◀ *Sicily* ▶

1 kg of sword fish, 500 g of tomato pulp, 1 onion, 1 clove of garlic, bay leaves, parsley, salted capers, white wine, white flour, extra virgin olive oil, salt.

Remove the skin from the fish and cut it into slices, flour it and fry it in a pan with abundant oil, remove it and drain it, leaving it to dry on absorbent paper and sprinkle it with a little salt.
Place an oven-proof dish on the hot ring, with grated onions and crushed garlic, a few broken up bay leaves, the tomato pulp, a pinch of salt and oil.
Cook for about twenty minutes, then remove from the heat and add the slices of fish, sprinkle with finely chopped parsley, adding a few whole capers and a drop of white wine.
Place in a moderately hot oven for about fifteen minutes before serving.

STEWED EEL
◀ *Veneto* ▶ 🔲

800 g of eel, 3 skinned tomatoes, 1 medium sized onion, 2 cloves of garlic, 1 spoonful of finely chopped parsley, 1 glass of white wine, corn flour (or coarse salt or breadcrumbs), 20 g of butter, vinegar, 3 spoonfuls extra virgin olive oil, salt, pepper in grains.

Rub the eel with the flour (or the coarse salt or the breadcrumbs), remove the innards and leave it to soak in water and vinegar for about half an hour. In the meantime, peel and grate the onion and the garlic.
Put the oil and the butter in a casserole and lightly fry the onion and the garlic; when they begin to brown, add the eel, cut into small pieces 5-6 cm big and floured.
Leave the fish pieces to brown gently, turn them over with a wooden spoon, add the white wine, allow this to

evaporate and, immediately afterwards, add the tomatoes which have had the skins and seeds removed.

Continue cooking for another 15 minutes, add salt to taste, flavour with freshly ground pepper, cover and cook a few more minutes.

Finally, add the finely chopped parsley, stir delicately and serve with yellow *polenta*.

STOCCAFISSO ALLA VICENTINA (VICENZA STYLE SALTED COD)
◀ *Veneto* ▶

1 kg of salted cod softened by soaking in water, 50 g of salted anchovies, 300 g of onions, 1 bunch of parsley, white flour, milk, extra virgin olive oil, salt, pepper.

In fact, this is the preparation for dried cod, not for salted cod (*stoccafisso*), but since this recipe is more commonly known by this name, we have used it.

Slice the onion thinly and fry gently in a few spoonfuls of oil; as soon as it is soft (but before changing colour) add the finely chopped parsley and the anchovies, well cleaned with the salt and scales removed.

Leave this sauce to become quite hot, stirring so that the anchovies disintegrate in the oil, then remove from the heat. Remove the skin and bones from the cod, cut it into pieces and flour lightly.

Lay it in an earthenware saucepan and cover it with the onion and anchovy sauce, and enough oil and milk in equal quantities to cover it completely. Cover the saucepan and cook on a low heat for at least 3 hours, shaking the saucepan by the handles every now and then. Serve with hot *polenta*.

LEGHORN *CACCIUCCO* (SPICY FISH SOUP)
◄ *Tuscany* ►

600 g of fish suitable for soup (complete fish), 800 g of sliced fish (dogfish, angler fish, mullet, etc.), 1 kg of molluscs (squids, octopus, cuttle-fish, etc.), 4-5 squills or mantis shrimps (one per person), 500 g of ripe tomatoes, 1 onion, 1 carrot, 1 stick of celery, 2 cloves of, 1 glass of red wine, parsley, extra virgin olive oil, salt, red peppercorn, slices of bread.

Clean all the various kinds of fish. Wash and mince together the onion, carrot and celery and fry lightly in abundant oil.
As soon as the onion begins to brown, add the octopus and the cuttlefish, cut roughly into pieces; after they have fried lightly, pour the wine over them. After about 10 minutes remove them from the saucepan, and add instead the tomatoes, with skins and seeds removed and cut into small cubes, the complete fish and their heads, if available, and add a few ladlefuls of hot broth or boiling water.
After cooking for 15-20 minutes, break up the fish and put it through a sieve, and immediately replace it on the heat.
At this point add the previously cooked molluscs, and if necessary add a little more hot water or broth, add salt and flavour with the peppercorn. After 20 minutes add the last fish kept aside (squills, mantis shrimps, the sliced fish) and cook for 20 more minutes; before removing from the heat add a generous handful of finely chopped parsley.
The *cacciucco* must be kept liquid and when the cooking is finished it is served in bowls in which toasted slices of bread have been placed.
For a variation on this recipe, use a glassful of vinegar instead of the red wine.

STUFFED SQUID
◄ *Friuli Venezia-Giulia* ►

8 cleaned squid, 2 cloves of, 1 egg (optional), 1 bunch of parsley, breadcrumbs, extra virgin olive oil, salt, pepper.

Clean, wash and dry the squid. Prepare the filling by mincing the tentacles of the squid together with the garlic and the parsley, add salt and pepper to taste, and lightly fry the mixture in oil, in which a few spoonfuls of breadcrumbs have

already been browned. If desired, when the mixture is warm an egg yolk can be added to bind.

Use the mixture to fill the bags of the squids, closing them with a tooth pick.

Roast them, suitably oiled and salted, under a hot grill.

SEA FOOD FRY
◀ *Veneto, Emilia Romagna* ▶

Small squids, small cuttlefish, grummets, mussels, shrimps, Norway lobsters, flour (or batter and/or marinade), lemon, olive oil, salt.

The sea food fry can be prepared in various ways, from the most digestible, with the fish only floured (and immediately browned in hot oil), to those which include the fish being marinated for a short time, or coked in a tasty batter.

We suggest here the most traditional way; it can be varied to taste and unusual combinations can be tried.

Clean and shell the mussels and the grummets, rinse the shrimps and the Norway lobsters under running water and dry them.

Clean the squids carefully; if they are small, leave them whole, otherwise cut them into strips, leaving the tufts whole, however.

Clean the cuttlefish and cut them into strips. Rinse the squids and the cuttlefish under cold running water and dry accurately. According to the type of procedure chosen for the frying, leave the fish to marinate or to stand in the batter. Fry the mixed fish in hot oil, dry on absorbent paper and sprinkle with salt.

PIKE IN SAUCE
◀ *Veneto* ▶ 📷

1 pike about 1 kg in weight, 1 carrot, ½ onion, 1 stick of celery, 1 glass of white wine, salt, pepper in grains.
<u>For the sauce</u>: 150 g of parsley, 150 g of salted anchovies, 150 g of capers, extra virgin olive oil.

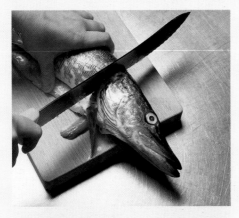

◆ Clean and gut the pike, wash it under running water and drain well.

◆ Boil the fish in a casserole in water flavoured with the wine and the vegetables, a few grains of pepper and salt.

◆ In the meantime prepare the sauce: mince finely the capers, the parsley and the anchovies (which has been boned and from which the salt has been removed with a damp cloth) and amalgamate the mixture with abundant oil. When the pike is cooked, delicately remove the bones, and place the meat in an oven-proof dish.

◆ Dress it with the sauce and leave it to stand for a time (if possible, overnight) for the flavours and the ingredients to blend: Serve accompanied by *polenta* freshly prepared or sliced and toasted on an open fire or under the grill.

mussels, and towards the end of the cooking add abundant finely chopped parsley. Serve the mussels together with their cooking liquid and lemon juice. This preparation can also be used to garnish spaghetti (in this case it is better to eliminate the shells).

OCTOPUS WITH PARSLEY
◀ *Sardinia* ▶

One large octopus weighing 1 kg, 1 lemon, 2 cloves of garlic, parsley, bay leaves, extra virgin olive oil, salt, pepper.

Clean the octopus and beat it to soften the meat (to be tender the octopus must have two rows of suckers). Bring a saucepan of water to the boil with a bay leaf, a garlic clove and salt; put the octopus in the saucepan and cook it for an hour: it will be cooked when the prongs of a fork can penetrate it easily. Remove from the heat and leave the octopus in the saucepan until it has cooled a little; drain it and cut it into evenly sized pieces; put the pieces in an earthenware bowl. Separately prepare a sauce, mixing the lemon juice with the oil, a mince of parsley and garlic, salt and pepper.
Dress the octopus with the sauce, mixing well, then leave it to stand in a cool place for at least 10 hours before bringing to the table.

BECCAFICU PILCHARDS
◀ *Sicily* ▶

1 kg of pilchards, 5 salted anchovies, 80 g of raisins, 80 g of pine kernels, 1 lemon, 1 bunch of parsley and basil, 1 sprig of bay leaves, 2 spoon-

LAKE WHITEFISH BAKED IN FOIL
◀ *Veneto* ▶

4 medium sized lake whitefish, 1 onion, 1 stick of celery, 1 carrot, 3 cloves of garlic, a few basil leaves, extra virgin olive oil, salt, pepper.

Clean the fish, wash and dry it and flavour it with salt and pepper. Mince together the vegetables, then oil a sheet of foil for each fish and put some of the minced vegetables on it. Stuff the fish with the rest of the vegetable mince, wrap them in foil and close well. Put the packets on an oven tray and cook in the oven for 4-5 minutes.

PEPPERED MUSSELS
◀ *Campania* ▶

2 kg of mussels, lemon juice, 1 sprig of parsley, pepper in grains.

After cleaning the mussels thoroughly, put them in a large covered pan on a high heat together with abundant freshly ground pepper. Shake the pan frequently by the handles to open the fuls of sugar, 150 g of breadcrumbs, extra virgin olive oil, salt, pepper.

Clean and bone the pilchards, opening them like a book, wash them and leave them to dry laid out on a cloth.
Eliminate the salt and any scales and mince them finely, then mix with the breadcrumbs which have been browned in a few spoonfuls of oil, the raisins, which have been softened in warm water and drained, the finely chopped parsley, the pine kernels, salt and pepper. Spread the mixture on the pilchards and roll them up, fixing them with a tooth pick.
Pour a little oil into an oven-proof dish and arrange the rolls in the dish, alternating them with bay leaves and dress with a sauce prepared by dissolving the sugar in the lemon juice and adding a few spoonfuls of oil. Cook in a hot oven at 200°C for about 20 minutes. Serve, dusted with finely chopped basil and with lemon segments.

BASS BAKED IN FOIL
◀ Sardinia ▶

1 bass about 250 g in weight, 2 potatoes, fresh tomatoes, 1 clove of garlic, rosemary, parsley, extra virgin olive oil, salt.

Remove the scales from the bass, gut it and clean it perfectly. Peel the tomatoes, eliminate the seeds and cut them into small cubes. Peel the potatoes and cut into thin slices.
Cover a tray with a sheet of foil, leaving enough overhanging to cover the contents. Lay the bass on the foil and put inside a pinch of salt, a sprig of parsley and a little rosemary; cover the bass

with the tomatoes and the potatoes; pour oil over it and dust it with salt, add a clove of garlic, and cover completely with the foil. Cook in a hot oven at 250°C for about half an hour.

GENOESE *STOCCAFISSO* (SALTED COD)
◀ *Liguria* ▶

1 kg of salted cod, 2 salted anchovies, 4 fresh mushrooms, 2 tomatoes, 1 onion, 1 carrot, 1 stick of celery, 1 clove of garlic, parsley, extra virgin olive oil, salt, pepper.

Mince the onion, garlic, carrot, celery and a sprig of parsley. Fry these lightly in a frying pan with abundant oil and then add the de-salted anchovies, breaking them up in the pan. Add the cod – which will have been left to soak for 24 hours – cut into pieces, add pepper and leave it to absorb the flavours for a few moments. Add the thinly sliced mushrooms and the fresh tomatoes, from which the seeds have been eliminated and which have been cut into small pieces; add salt to taste and cook on a moderate heat until the cod is perfectly cooked through.

SIDE
DISHES

ASPARAGUS WITH MELTED BUTTER
◀ *Piedmont* ▶

500 g of asparagus, 1 sprig of sage, nutmeg, grated Parmesan cheese, 50 g of butter, salt.

Eliminate the hard part of the asparagus stems, wash them and tie into bunches.
Arrange them standing vertically in a saucepan and fill the saucepan with water up to two thirds the height of the stems. Add salt and cover the saucepan, bring to the boil and cook for 20-30 minutes.
Remove the asparagus from the saucepan and leave them in a colander to drain. Melt the butter in a frying pan, flavour with the sage and a pinch of grated nutmeg, and brown gently. Lay the asparagus on an oven-proof plate, pour over them the flavoured oil and dust with abundant grated Parmesan cheese, put in a hot oven for a couple of minutes, and then serve.

CAPONATA
◀ *Sicily* ▶

4 aubergines, 4 large, firm, ripe tomatoes, 100 g of black olives, $\frac{1}{2}$ stick of celery, 1 onion, 1 clove of garlic, 50 g of salted capers, apple vinegar, extra virgin olive oil, coarse salt and fine salt.

Clean the aubergines and cut them in cubes, sprinkle coarse salt over them and leave them to drain for half an hour in a colander. In the meantime, slice the onion thinly, crush the garlic, peel the tomatoes (after tossing them into boiling water for a moment) and pass them through a sieve, remove the stones from the olives and cut them roughly into pieces, and clean and slice the celery.
Put all the ingredients in a saucepan with a little oil, add the washed capers and cook on a moderate heat until it becomes a dense sauce. Drain the aubergines to eliminate the liquid, fry them in oil and add them to the sauce, leaving it to cook for another ten minutes. Before removing from the heat, add salt to taste and a few drops of vinegar. Serve the caponata preferably cold.

ARTICHOKES *ALLA GIUDIA*
◀ *Lazio* ▶

4 artichokes, 1 bunch of parsley, a few leaves of fresh mint, extra virgin olive oil, salt.

Cut the points off the artichokes, remove the outer leaves, cut off the stems, wash, drain and dry them. Open the leaves in the centre a little, put a little finely chopped parsley and mint and a pinch of salt inside.

Arrange the artichokes in a small casserole, so that they remain upright, one against the other, pour oil in the casserole to half way up the artichokes and put it on the hot ring.

Cook on a high heat, without a cover and, when the leaves have become dark and are crusty, put the lid on the casserole and continue cooking for a few minutes on a moderate heat. Drain them and arrange them on a serving plate.

FRIED ARTICHOKES
◀ *The Marches* ▶

6 fairly large and tender artichokes, 3 eggs, flour, lemon, oil for frying, salt, pepper.

Clean the artichokes, removing the stems, the hard outer leaves and the points; cut them into segments and leave them in a little water and lemon juice.

Beat the eggs with a pinch of salt and pepper, dry the artichokes and flour them, then put them in the egg; fry them in abundant hot oil.

BRINDISI CARDOONS
◀ *Puglia* ▶

1 kg cardoons, capers, 80 g of black olives, 4 de-boned anchovies, parsley, 1 lemon, breadcrumbs, extra virgin olive oil, salt, pepper.

Clean the cardoons and cut them into sticks of equal length. Boil them for about an hour in salted water and the juice of the lemon; drain them and dry them, and arrange them in layers in a lightly oiled baking tray.

Between one layer and another, place a few capers, the stoned black olives, the anchovies cut into small pieces, the finely chopped parsley, salt and pepper.

Complete the last layer with a dribble of oil and a dusting of breadcrumbs.

Cook in a moderately hot oven until they are nicely golden.

BITTER-SWEET SMALL ONIONS
◀ *Emilia Romagna* ▶

450 g of small white onions, $\frac{1}{2}$ glassful of balsamic vinegar, 40 g of sugar, 7 spoonfuls of extra virgin olive oil, 60 g of butter, salt.

117

Peel the onions, wash them and dry carefully. Put them into a pan and place the pan on a moderate heat; when they begin to turn gold, add the butter and the oil and fry, turning them continually with a wooden spoon.

Pour over the vinegar, allow this to evaporate almost completely, then add the sugar, lower the heat, cover the pan and continue cooking, adding a little hot water if necessary.

After about half an hour, stir the onions around again and continue cooking for another 30 minutes.

At this point the liquid in the pan should be neither too liquid nor too dense, and it should be poured over the onions at the moment of serving.

SAUERKRAUT
◀ Trentino Alto-Adige ▶

1 kg of milk fermented sauerkraut, 3 cloves of garlic, broth, extra virgin olive oil, salt.

Heat the oil, add the crushed garlic cloves and brown gently, removing them as soon as they begin to darken. Rinse the sauerkraut rapidly under running water, drain it and put it in the oil for a few minutes to take on the flavour.
Cover it with broth or hot water, add salt and cook on a low heat in a covered pan, stirring from time to time.
The secret of sauerkraut depends on its slow cooking; when it becomes golden brown it is ready.
The sauerkraut goes extremely well with frankfurters, one of the gastronomic couples typical of the Alto Adige region.

POTATO CROQUETTES
◆

700 g of potatoes, 1 egg, flour, 1 dl of single cream, 50 g of butter, salt.

Wash and boil the potatoes in salted water, then peel them and mash them adding a knob of butter.
Put them in a saucepan and heat to dry them out, stirring continuously with a wooden spoon.
Add the cream and the egg yolks, add salt to taste and leave to cool.
Form balls 2 cm in diameter with this mixture, roll them in flour and fry them in butter till they are golden brown.

BEANS AL FIASCO WITH OIL
◀ Tuscany ▶ 📷

350 g of shelled Cannelloni beans, 6 sage leaves, 2 cloves of garlic, 1/2 glass of extra virgin olive oil, salt, pepper.

This is a very old recipe, and requires time and patience. First procure an empty 2 litre glass flask, remove the outer straw lining and wash the flask thoroughly. Fill it two thirds full with beans, then add the oil, the roughly minced sage leaves, the crushed garlic and 2 glassfuls of water.
Cork the flask using the straw of the lining, or cotton or something similar, but without pressing tightly, so that the water can evaporate during the cooking.
At this point the Tuscan peasants used to place the flask upright on the hot embers, covered with warm cinders, leaving it to cook for at least 5 hours or even overnight. In the absence of an open fire, put the flask in a deep baking tray in a moderate oven, and cook with the bain-marie method.
The beans will be ready when all the water has evaporated from the flask and the legumes have absorbed the oil completely. Remove the beans from the flask, add salt and plenty of pepper, then dress them with so much extra virgin olive oil that they are practically drowned in it.

BEANS ALL'UCCELLETTO WITH TOMATO
◀ Tuscany ▶

500 g of fresh beans, 5-6 sage leaves, 6 spoonfuls of tomato purée, extra virgin olive oil, salt.

frying pan and gently fry in oil. As soon as they begin to brown, add the beans, rinsed and drained, add half a glass of water and salt, and continue cooking for about half an hour.

FRIED COURGETTE FLOWERS

◆

16 courgette flowers, 2 eggs, nutmeg, 150 g of flour, ¹/₂ glass of dry white wine, 8-10 spoonfuls of extra virgin olive oil, salt, pepper.

Boil the beans in plenty of salted water, adding salt towards the end of the cooking; then drain them.
Lightly fry the sage leaves in an oiled pan on a low heat for a few minutes. Add the beans and the tomato purée, add salt to taste and leave it on a moderate heat for 10 minutes to absorb the flavour, stirring continuously. When the tomato purée has completely dried, the beans will be ready.
Add a little raw oil, mix well and serve.

BROAD BEANS
◀ *Abruzzo* ▶

600 g of fresh shelled broad beans, 100 g of pig's cheek, 1 onion, extra virgin olive oil, salt.

Clean the broad beans, leaving them in a bowl of cold water for a few minutes, to eliminate impurities and bad beans that will float to the surface.
Put the finely sliced onion and the pig's cheek cut into small pieces in a

Put the flour and the egg yolks into a mixing bowl with salt, pepper and grated nutmeg.
Mix together and add the wine gradually, then leave to stand for about half an hour.
After this time, add to the mixture the stiffly beaten egg whites. Cut the stems off the flowers and remove the inner pistils by twisting them, then put each flower into the batter mixture, so that they are well covered. Heat the oil in a large frying pan and fry the flowers for a few minutes until they are golden brown.
Place them on absorbent kitchen paper, to eliminate excess grease, sprinkle with a pinch of salt and serve.

STUFFED AUBERGINES
◀ *Puglia* ▶

4 large firm aubergines, 100 g of Bologna sausage, 2 firm, ripe tomatoes, 2 eggs, breadcrumbs, 1 handful of grated sheep's milk cheese, extra virgin olive oil, salt, pepper.

Cut the aubergines in half lengthwise and remove the pulp in the centre. This must be minced together with the tomatoes and cooked in a little oil with salt and pepper for about twenty minutes.

Then add the beaten eggs, the sheep's milk cheese, a small amount of bread-crumbs and the minced Bologna sausage.

Mix well and put the mixture into the hollow aubergine skins, arrange on an oiled baking tray, dress again with the cheese, salt and pepper.

Pour a little water 1 cm deep into the tray, then cook in a moderate oven for about an hour and a half.

POTATOES WITH LARD
◄ Emilia Romagna ►

500 g of potatoes which are not floury, 100 g of fresh lard, 1 onion, 1 spoonful of finely chopped parsley, 2 spoonfuls of flour, 1 glassful of meat broth, $^1/_2$ glassful of dry white wine, 40 g of butter, salt, pepper in grains.

Cut the lard into small cubes, put them into a small saucepan, cover them with water and boil for just a minute, drain them and place them in cold water, drain again, then leave to dry on a clean cloth.

Peel the potatoes, wash them and dry them carefully and cut them into segments.

Put the lard in a casserole, add the butter and fry gently, stirring every now and then, until the lard has melted. At this point, add the peeled thinly sliced onion and cook until it softens, then add the flour, which must be lightly browned.

Add the broth and the white wine and, stirring continuously with a wooden spoon, bring to the boil, then finally add the potatoes. Flavour with salt and freshly ground pepper, bring to a fast boil then reduce the heat considerably, cover and continue cooking for just over half an hour.

Drain the potatoes, put them on a hot serving plate and sprinkle over the finely chopped parsley, then serve immediately.

POTATOES IN TUNA SAUCE
◆

5-6 medium sized potatoes, 200 g of tuna fish in oil, 1 lemon, 2 cloves of garlic, 1 sprig of parsley, paprika, extra virgin olive oil, salt.

Boil the potatoes and in the meantime prepare the sauce: drain the oil from the tuna fish and break the fish up with a fork, add a few drops of lemon juice, a pinch of paprika, the minced garlic and parsley and mix well together with a generous quantity of oil.

Drain the potatoes, peel them and cut them into slices; spread the sauce on them and serve.

121

PEPERONATA
◀ *Puglia* ▶ 🔳

500 g of red and yellow sweet peppers, 2 large onions, 400 g of tomatoes, basil, 2 spoonfuls of capers, 1 pinch of marjoram, extra virgin olive oil, salt, pepper.

Scorch the peppers on the flames to remove the outer skin. Open them and remove the seeds and the white strips. Clean and peel the tomatoes (tossing them into boiling water for a moment) and cut them into pieces.
Slice the onions and cook them in a deep pan with a little oil; add the peppers, the tomatoes, the capers, a few basil leaves, a pinch of marjoram and, lastly, salt and pepper. Cook slowly for about three quarters of an hour, stirring occasionally. *Peperonata* can be served hot or cold.

PEAS WITH HAM
◀ *Lazio* ▶

1 kg of fresh peas, 150 g of raw ham, 1 sprig of parsley, broth, butter, extra virgin olive oil, salt, pepper.

Put the thinly sliced onions, some oil and a knob of butter into a casserole and heat.
As soon as the onion is soft, add the peas, salt and pepper, and pour on some broth or hot water. Just before finishing the cooking, add the raw ham cut into cubes and the finely chopped parsley.
An alternative is to substitute the raw ham with cooked ham. The peas prepared this way can also be used to dress *tagliatelle* pasta.

TOMATOES AU GRATIN
◀ *Umbria* ▶

4 firm, ripe tomatoes, 1 bunch of parsley, 2 cloves of garlic, the pulp of some black olives, breadcrumbs, extra virgin olive oil, salt, red peppercorn.

Wash the tomatoes, cut them in half and remove the seeds; salt them inside and leave them to drain, placing them upside down on a sloping surface.
Crush the garlic and finely chop the parsley, and add a few spoonfuls of the olive pulp and a generous dose of breadcrumbs, mixing well together.
Pour a little oil flavoured with salt and a pinch of paprika on the mixture, then use it to fill the tomatoes arranged on an oiled baking tray.
Sprinkle with a little breadcrumbs and pour a dribble of oil over them. Cook in a moderate oven for about half an hour, then turn up the heat and cook for 10 more minutes to brown the top. If desired, the filling can be enriched with capers and salted anchovies, and they can be garnished with green or black olives. Accompany the tomatoes with boiled brown rice to present a tasty and nutritious one-course meal.

TRUFFLED BOLETE MUSHROOMS WITH GARLIC AND PARSLEY
◆

500 g of fresh bolete mushrooms, 1-2 cloves of garlic, 1 bunch of parsley, 50 g of butter, 4 spoonfuls extra virgin olive oil, salt, pepper.

Clean the bolete mushrooms thoroughly and slice them thinly. Put some oil, the butter and the garlic in a casserole and fry lightly, add the bolete mushrooms together with the finely chopped parsley.
Add salt and pepper, cover the pan and cook slowly until completely cooked. If the mushrooms become too dry, add a little hot water to moisten them. This is the basic preparation, not only for bolete mushrooms, but also for many other kinds of mushrooms. The garlic can be used either in whole cloves or crushed, and in this case half a clove can be enough.

RED RADISHES IN *SAÓR*
◀ *Veneto* ▶ 🔲

8 red Trevisan radish heads, 150 g of onions, 40 g of raisins, 30 g of pine kernels, 1 spoonful of sugar, $1/2$ glassful of red wine vinegar, 3 spoonfuls of extra virgin olive oil, salt, pepper in grains.

Wash the raisins and leave them to soak in cold water for an hour. Peel and slice the onions thinly, put them in a frying pan with the oil and fry softly for a few minutes on a medium heat, stirring them with a wooden spoon.
Add the vinegar and the sugar, mix together, add the drained raisins and the pine kernels, allow the liquid to evaporate, then remove from heat. Clean the radishes carefully, wash them and dry them with a manual salad dryer, and cut every head in quarters lengthwise.
Add the radishes to the frying pan and let them cook on a moderate heat,

mixing from time to time. Before serving, add salt and freshly ground pepper to taste.

FRENCH BEAN FLAN
◆

400 g of French beans, 2 eggs, ginger, coriander seeds, breadcrumbs, 150 g of grated Parmesan cheese, extra virgin olive oil, salt.

The French beans should be of the type without strings. Wash them and boil them in salted water for 20 minutes. Drain them and finish cooking them on a high heat, after placing them in a casserole with some oil. Remove them from the heat, add the eggs, flavour with salt, a little grated ginger and freshly ground coriander seeds; mix well and add the Parmesan. Transfer the mixture to a baking tray lightly oiled and sprinkled with breadcrumbs, and put into the oven at 180°C approx. for half an hour.

PUMPKIN FLAN
◆

1 kg pumpkin, 3 eggs, nutmeg, ginger, paprika, breadcrumbs, $1/2$ glassful of single cream, 100 g of grated Parmesan cheese, butter, salt.

Remove the rind and the seeds from the pumpkin, cut it in pieces and cook it in the oven.
When it is cooked, mash it in a vegetable masher, collecting the purée in a mixing bowl. Add two whole eggs and one yolk, the Parmesan, the cream, a few spoonfuls of breadcrumbs, salt, a pinch of paprika, one of grated nutmeg and a little freshly ground ginger. Grease an oven-proof

Prepare a marinade mixing half a glass of oil with a pinch of salt, a pinch of paprika, the crushed garlic, and the washed and chopped basil. Clean, wash and dry the courgettes and cut them in half lengthwise, cover them with the marinade and leave them for about half an hour.

Remove the courgettes from the marinade and drain them, then place them on the grill.

Brown them for about 7 minutes each side, pouring a little marinade over them from time to time, remove them from the grill and lay them on absorbent paper to remove the excess oil and serve very hot.

dish, sprinkle breadcrumbs over it, put the mixture into it, place a few knobs of butter on top and put it in the oven to cook at about 160°C for three quarters of an hour.

VEGETABLE PIE
◀ *The Marches* ▶

700 g of potatoes, 1 onion, 3 large sweet peppers (2 yellow and 1 red), 400 g of ripe tomatoes, marjoram, extra virgin olive oil, salt, pepper.

Clean, wash and slice the vegetables, keeping them separate. Place them in a greased baking tray, arranging them in layers, alternating the flavours and dressing each layer with oil, salt, pepper and marjoram. Cook in a hot oven for about an hour, then remove and leave to stand for a few minutes before serving.

GARLIC COURGETTES
◆

6 courgettes, 3 cloves of garlic, basil, paprika, extra virgin olive oil, salt.

DESSERTS

BABÀ AL RUM
◀ Sicily ▶

<u>For the dough</u>: 300 g of flour, 100 g of butter, 5 eggs, 1 lemon, 1 coffee cup of warm milk, 1 spoonful of sugar, 25 g of yeast, salt.
<u>For the syrup</u>: 300 g of sugar, 1 glass of rum, apricot jam, 1 lemon.

To prepare the dough for the babà, mix together in a mixing bowl the butter, softened and cut into small pieces, the eggs and the sugar; add the flour little by little and a pinch of salt and, lastly, the grated rind of the lemon and the yeast dissolved in the warm milk.

Mix thoroughly and when the dough is of the consistency that it comes away from the sides of the bowl easily cover it and leave it to stand for an hour in a warm place.

After this time, knead the dough for a few minutes, then divide it and put it into the special babà moulds, previously greased and floured; cover them with a cloth and leave them to rise until they have doubled in volume. Cook in a hot oven for about half an hour.

In the meantime, to prepare the liquid in which the babàs will be soaked, melt the sugar over the heat with 5 dl of water and the lemon rind until it forms a syrup; remove from the heat and add the rum. Pour this liquid over the babàs while they are still warm and let it soak in; finally, add a little water to the apricot jam, heat briefly and brush the surfaces of the babàs with this mixture.

FRUIT BOATS
◆

<u>For the sweet pastry</u>: 200 g of flour, 100 g of butter, 2 eggs, salt.
<u>For the filling</u>: 100 g of strawberries, 100 g of red currants, 100 g of raspberries, 100 g of gooseberries, custard cream, 2 lemons, 2 spoonfuls of sugar, olive oil, flour.

Make a mound of the flour and the sugar. In the centre make a well and put the butter, softened and cut into small pieces, a whole egg and a pinch of salt. Quickly work the dough until it is soft and of an even texture. Leave it to stand covered by a cloth for half an hour.

In the meantime, clean and rinse the fruit quickly under running water, dry it with a cloth and put it on a plate, keeping the different kinds separate. Powder it with sugar, spray on the juice of the lemons and leave it to steep in a cool place, stirring from time to time. Roll out the dough with a rolling pin to a thickness of a few millimetres. Prepare the boat shaped moulds (or round moulds) one next to the other on the work surface, brush them lightly with oil.

At this point, roll the pastry around the rolling pin and lay it on top of the moulds. Make it stick to the edges of the moulds by pressing it with the fingers on to the edges of the moulds, pass the rolling pin across so that it is cut around the edges of the moulds.

Re-knead the left-over pieces of dough and repeat the operation with more moulds, and continue until all the dough is used up. Prick the pastry in each mould with a fork and line each pastry case with a piece of greaseproof paper; fill these with a layer of dry lentils.

Cook the boats in a hot oven for about a quarter of an hour, remove from the oven, discard the lentils and the paper linings, and delicately remove the boats from the moulds. Leave them to dry on a grid.

Then place a few spoonfuls of custard cream into each boat, and place the fruit on top of this. The boats can be sprinkled with icing sugar when served, or the surfaces can be made shiny with a jam icing.

BECCUTE
◀ The Marches ▶

600 g of flour, 100 g of pine kernels, 100 g of walnut kernels, 80 g of peeled almonds, 100 g of raisins, 100 g of dried figs, 100 g of sugar, extra virgin olive oil, salt.

Put the dried figs in warm water to soften and, separately, also the raisins; roughly mince the walnuts and the almonds. Mix the flour with 4 spoonfuls of oil, the sugar, a pinch of salt, 1 drained fig cut into small pieces, the raisins well squeezed, the pine kernels, the walnuts and the almonds. Add, little by little, some warm water, until the mixture is soft and of an even texture. Divide the dough into small portions, and make them into little rolls. Oil a baking tray and place the beccute on it in rows. Cook in a medium hot oven for half an hour.

COFFEE CREAM PUFFS
◆

For the puffs: 150 g of flour, 120 g of butter, 5 eggs, salt, 15 g of sugar.
For the filling: 1 dl of coffee, 4 eggs, 125 g of sugar, 3 dl of milk, 40 g of corn flour, finely ground coffee.

In a deep sided pan bring to the boil 350 g of water, the butter, a pinch of salt and the sugar. When it begins to boil, remove from the heat and quickly pour in the flour, stirring with a wooden spoon. Put the pan back on the heat, bring it back to the boil and, stirring continuously, cook it for about 8 minutes, until the mixture comes away from the sides of the pan. Remove the pan from the heat and add the first egg to the mixture, mixing it in very quickly. After having amalgamated the first egg with the mixture, and not before, add the second, and so on until the last. At this point the dough will be as soft as a cream. Fill an icing bag with the

129

mixture and squirt little balls as big as walnuts onto a buttered baking tray at a distance of 3 cm from each other. Put into the oven and cook at 180°C for about 15 minutes.

Heat the milk and the coffee, mix the egg yolks with the sugar, add the corn oil, possibly dissolved in a little coffee. Mix to form a soft cream, then add the milk and the coffee very gradually, continuing to stir all the time; bring this mixture to the boil on a moderate heat. Remove from the heat and as soon as the cream has cooled, add a pinch of very finely ground coffee; fill the puffs with this mixture and cover them with a sugar icing, to which a little coffee has been added.

ANISEED BISCUITS

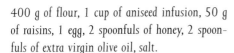

400 g of flour, 1 cup of aniseed infusion, 50 g of raisins, 1 egg, 2 spoonfuls of honey, 2 spoonfuls of extra virgin olive oil, salt.

Wash the raisins and leave them to soak in a little warm water. In the meantime, make the flour into a mound and into a well in the centre place the egg, the honey and a pinch of salt. Begin to knead the dough, adding little by little, the aniseed infusion. After kneading the dough for about ten minutes, beat the drained raisins in a food mixer, and add them to the dough, always continuing to knead. Leave it to stand for about half an hour, then roll it out with a rolling pin to a thickness of approx. 3-4 mm, then cut it into rectangles. Lay the biscuits thus obtained on a lightly oiled and floured baking tray and bake in a hot oven for about 20 minutes.

BÔNET (ALMOND AND CHOCOLATE BLANCMANGE)
◀ *The Aosta Valley, Piedmont* ▶

8 eggs, 1 l of milk, 3 spoonfuls of cocoa powder, 7 almond macaroons, 250 g of sugar, 1 spoonful of Marsala wine, 1 lemon.

Beat the egg yolks in a bowl with 8 spoonfuls of sugar. Add the cocoa, the stiffly beaten egg whites and the grated rind of the lemon mixed with the crumbled macaroons and the Marsala wine. Pour the remaining sugar into a ring shaped blancmange mould, heat this to caramelise the sugar, then fill the mould with the egg mixture. Cook with the bain-marie method in the oven for about 3 hours on a very low heat. The water around the blancmange mould must hardly boil: the blancmange will be ready when a tooth pick pushed in comes out clean and dry.

Leave to cool, then leave the dessert in the refrigerator for at least 4 hour before turning it out of the mould and serving.

CANNOLI (SWEET PASTRY ROLLS)
◀ *Sicily* ▶

250 g of ricotta cheese, 200 g of flour, 50 g of candied oranges and limes, 30 g of dark bitter chocolate, 20 g of butter, 1 spoonful of sugar, 1 spoonful of un-sweetened cocoa, 1 spoonful of instant coffee, dry white wine, 1 egg, olive oil, salt.

To prepare these sweet Sicilian pastry rolls, use a special metal cylinder around which to wrap the dough, available from household goods shops.

On the work surface, make a mound of the flour mixed with the cocoa, the coffee, the sugar and a pinch of salt; make a well in the centre and add the softened butter cut into small pieces and knead the dough adding enough white wine to make it soft and elastic. Wrap the dough in a cloth and leave it to stand for about an hour in a cool, dark place.

In the meantime, prepare the filling, mixing the ricotta cheese with the sugar, the candied fruit cut into small pieces and the chocolate, grated with a knife; mix well together and leave in the refrigerator. Roll out the dough to a thickness of a few millimetres, cut circles about 10 cm in diameter and work them into oval shapes. Wrap each oval around the special metal cylinder, greased with oil, and press together at the point where the pastry overlaps to form cylinders, sealing them with a little egg white. Heat the oil in a deep pan and brown the *cannoli* evenly.

Drain and dry on absorbent paper; after a few minutes remove the metal cylinders and repeat the operation with more pastry ovals, until they are all cooked. When all the *cannoli* are cooked and cooled, fill them with the ricotta cream and serve them, dusting them with a little icing sugar.

To prepare the flaky pastry use chilled utensils and ice cold water. Mix the flour with a pinch of salt and a cup of ice cold water until the dough is firm, then leave it to stand, covered by a cloth, in a cool, dark place.

With wet fingers, knead the butter until it is of the same consistency as the dough, then make it into a rectangular shape.

Roll out the pastry on a well floured work surface and in the centre place the butter; fold the dough in three over the butter to make a packet and press it lightly with the rolling pin to incorporate the butter, leave it to stand for 5 minutes.

Now begin the folding phase of the pastry, necessary to produce a fragrant and crumbly.

Keep the flour at hand to maintain the work surface and the rolling pin well floured. Roll out the dough into a rectangle 1 cm thick, fold in three again in the other direction and roll it out again, then repeat this procedure again, then leave it for about 15 minutes in the refrigerator. Repeat the procedure twice more (the folds must be repeated six times in all), then the flaky pastry is ready.

To prepare the *cannoncini* use a special metal cone (available in household goods shops) which give this dessert their particular shape. Roll out the

131

CANNONCINI (SMALL CANNONS)

◆

For the flaky pastry : 200 g of flour, 200 g of butter, 1 egg, salt.
For the filling: whipped cream or custard cream.

pastry with the rolling pin into a rectangle about 45 cm long and a few millimetres thick. From this, cut strips lengthwise about 3 cm wide.

Cut the end off each strip, then brush with egg white.

Place the end of a strip on the point of the cylinder and wrap the strip around the cylinder, so that the edge of the strip overlaps as it winds round the metal cone.

Arrange the cones on the baking tray, leaving room for them to expand during cooking; put the baking tray in the refrigerator for a quarter of an hour. Brush the surface of the cannelloni with egg white and sprinkle with sugar. Pre-heat the oven and when it is hot cook the cannelloni for about 20 minutes.

Leave them to cool on a grid then remove the metal cones. Cannelloni are usually filled with custard cream, but they are excellent with a filling of just whipped cream, or with chocolate or coffee flavoured cream.

CANTUCCINI
◀ Tuscany ▶ 📷

300 g of flour, 200 g of sugar, 100 g of sweet almonds, 3 eggs, 1 spoonful of grated orange rind, 1 spoonful of aniseeds, 3 g of bicarbonate of soda, butter, salt.

Form a mound of the flour, sifted together with the bicarbonate of soda, on the pastry board.

Make a well in the centre and put in it the sugar, a pinch of slat, the orange rind (not the white part), the aniseeds and the almonds with their skins.

Break the two eggs into it and mix well, adding a little milk if the mixture is too dry.

Form three strings as thick as two fingers together and brush them with the egg yolk.

Cook in the oven at 190° C for a quarter of an hour, then remove and cut it diagonally, to form the classic cantuccini shape, then put back into the oven for 5 minutes.

SICILIAN CASSATA
◀ Sicily ▶

For the sponge: 150 g of flour, 150 g of sugar, 25 g of butter, 5 eggs, salt.

For the filling and to garnish: 500 g of ricotta cheese, 300 g of mixed candied fruit, 250 g of sugar, 200 g of apricot jam, 100 g of plain chocolate, 2 spoonfuls shelled pistachios, 1 small glassful of Maraschino wine, 1 glassful of orange flower water, 1 stick of vanilla.

To prepare the sponge: mix the sugar and the egg yolks together thoroughly until they form a soft cream, then add the flour gradually, stirring all the time, for about 15 minutes.

At this point work the butter, melted with the bain-marie method, and the salt.

Whip the egg whites stiffly and, one spoonful at a time, gently stir them into the dough.

Pour it into a cake tin (according to tradition, this should be rectangular) and cook it in a hot oven for half an hour, until it comes easily away from the sides of the tin.

Let it cool and then cut it into slices about 1 cm thick and use them to line a rectangular or round mould,

previously lined with greased paper. Brush the surface of the sponge pieces with the jam, previous melted on a hot ring with a little orange flower water.

Heat the sugar until it melts, together with half a glass of water and the vanilla; when it has the consistency of a syrup, leave it to cool, remove the vanilla stick and mix in the ricotta cheese, stirring it well with a wooden spoon, in order to obtain a smooth cream without lumps.

Mix this cream with the candied fruit cut into small cubes, the chocolate cut into little pieces, the pistachios (tossed into boiling water and then well dried) and the Maraschino.

Pour the ricotta mixture into a mould and knock this on the work surface in order to eliminate air bubbles in the dessert. Put in the fridge to chill for at least a couple of hours.

Turn out the dessert with great care and cover it with an icing prepared with the apricot jam and the orange flower water.

Put it back in the refrigerator and serve well chilled.

CASTAGNACCIO (CHESTNUT DESSERT)
◀ *Tuscany* ▶

300 g of chestnut flour, 50 g of raisins, 30 g of pine kernels, extra virgin olive oil, salt.

Put the raisins in warm water to soften; in the meantime, mix the chestnut flour with water to obtain a soft, thick mixture.

Add the pine kernels, the drained and squeezed raisins and a pinch of salt; mix well, adding a few spoonfuls of extra virgin olive oil. Lightly oil a baking tray and dust it with breadcrumbs, pour the mixture onto it and cook in a moderate oven for about 40 minutes.

The chestnut bread will be ready when a dark crust that tends to crack has formed on top

Other ingredients, such as an apple cut into small cubes, fennel seeds, carob flour, rosemary, etc.

BOLOGNESE DOUGHNUTS
◀ *Emilia Romagna* ▶ 📷

400 g of flour, 150 g of sugar, 100 g of milk, 80 g of butter, 3 eggs, 20 g of baking powder for cakes, granulated sugar, salt.

Mix the flour with the sugar, the baking powder and a pinch of salt; make it into a mound with a well in the middle on the work surface; put the milk, the previously softened butter, cut up into small pieces, and 2 eggs in the well. Without kneading too much, work the ingredients to obtain a soft dough. Arrange the dough in doughnut shapes on a buttered baking tray

and dust with flour. Make a cut in the surface of each doughnut, brush the surface with an egg yolk, and sprinkle granulated sugar over them.

Cook in a moderately hot oven for about half an hour, until the surface is golden brown.

One of the many variations is with the addition of a teaspoonful of Grappa to the dough.

CICERCHIATA
◀ *Puglia* ▶

500 g of flour, 500 g of honey, 4 eggs, 200 dl of extra virgin olive oil, almonds, powdered cinnamon, sugar, chocolate flakes, olive oil, salt.

Prepare a dough mixing the flour, the eggs, the oil, 4 spoonfuls of sugar and a pinch of salt, to obtain a soft dough: the flour must absorb the oil evenly.

Divide the dough and work it to form long cylinders, cut them into pieces 1 cm long, form them into a shape similar to *gnocchi* passing them lightly – pushing with a finger – and rapidly across a cheese grater.

Fry them in hot oil just long enough for them to become golden, and in the meantime, heat the honey in a small saucepan until it become golden brown. Put the fried pieces of

dough into the honey and when they are well covered put them all on a large plate, arranging them in the shape of a doughnut.

Decorate with pieces of toasted almonds, flaked chocolate, ground cinnamon and sugar.

CREAM CHEESE TART
◆

For the sweet pastry: 200 g of flour, 100 g of sugar, 100 butter, 2 eggs, salt
For the ricotta cream: 500 g of ricotta cheese, 150 g of sugar, 1 egg, 1 lemon, 2 spoonfuls of candied fruit, 2 spoonfuls of raising, flour.

Make a mound of the flour mixed with the sugar. In the centre pour the softened butter cut into small pieces, a whole egg, an egg yolk and a pinch of salt.

Knead quickly until the dough is soft and even. Leave it to stand covered by a cloth for half an hour.

Use two thirds to line a cake tin and pour into this the filling obtained by mixing well the ricotta with the sugar, the egg, the grated lemon rind, the candied fruit and the raisins, previously softened in warm water and covered with flour.

With the remaining

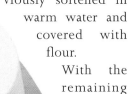

dough make strips and place them like a grid on top of the filling. Bake in a hot oven for about 40 minutes.

APPLE FAGGOTS

◆

<u>For the dough</u>: 250 g of flour, 1 egg, 2 spoonfuls of extra virgin olive oil, salt.
<u>For the filling</u>: 1 $\frac{1}{2}$ kg apples, 150 g of dry biscuits, 50 g of raisins, 20 g of pine kernels, 25 walnut kernels, $\frac{1}{2}$ glass of apple juice, $\frac{1}{2}$ spoonful of barley malt syrup, 1 lemon, 1 spoonful of honey, 1 pinch of cinnamon.

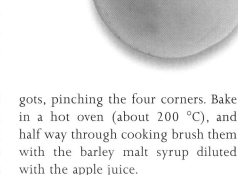

Add a pinch of salt to the flour and form a mound. Make a well in the centre and put the egg and the oil into it; knead it adding little by little enough water to give the dough the right consistency.

Knead it vigorously until it becomes smooth and elastic, then make it into a ball, put a little oil on it and leave it to stand for half an hour.

In the meantime, wash the raisins and leave them to soak, peel the apples and cut them into thin slices, grind the nuts.

Put the apples and the raisins (after draining and squeezing the water out of them) into a bowl, add the honey, cinnamon, pine kernels and the grated rind of the lemon, mix thoroughly, and leave to steep.

When this mixture is ready, roll out the dough with a rolling pin to obtain a thin pastry.

Cut it in 10 cm squares and then, using a spoon, put a little filling on each one and crumble a little of the biscuits on top. Dampen the edges with a little water and close the faggots, pinching the four corners. Bake in a hot oven (about 200 °C), and half way through cooking brush them with the barley malt syrup diluted with the apple juice.

When the surfaces are golden brown, remove from the oven. Serve hot or cold.

137

FRUSTINGOLO
◀ *The Marches* ▶

200 g of flour, 1 kg of dried figs, 400 g of raisins, 1 kg of walnuts, 500 g of almonds, 100 g of plain chocolate, 200 g of sugar, 1 glassful of extra virgin olive oil.

Wash the dried figs and the raisins and soften them in a little warm water; in the meantime, shell the walnuts and the almonds.

Cut the chocolate, the figs, the walnuts and the almonds into small pieces, then mix all the ingredients in a bowl, adding them one by one.

Stir well and put into a greased cake tin. Bake for an hour.

GALÀNI
◀ *Veneto*

300 g of flour, 2 eggs, 2 oranges, 50 g of butter, icing sugar, olive oil, salt.

Mix thoroughly the eggs with the flour and the juice of the 2 oranges, adding the butter previously melted with the bain-marie method, and a pinch of salt.
Roll out this dough, then cut into rather large squares or diamond shapes (4x10) and fry them in hot oil until they are golden brown.
Drain the *galàni* and leave them to dry on absorbent kitchen paper. Before serving dust them with icing sugar.

GUBANA
◀ *Friuli Venezia-Giulia* ▶

For the dough: 600 g of flour, 450 g of sugar, 100 g of whole milk, 90 g of butter, 6 eggs, 1 lemon, 1 small glassful of rum, salt.
For the filling: 250 g of shelled and peeled walnuts, 250 g of sultanas, 150 g of pine kernels, 100 g of sugar, 300 g of cocoa, 1 small glass of rum, 1 small glass of Grappa, nutmeg, $^1/_2$ teaspoonful of ground cinnamon, butter.
To complete: 1 egg, sugar.

Prepare a rising batter by dissolving the yeast in the warm milk and adding 3 spoonfuls of flour.
Leave to rise in a warm, dark place, then add the butter, previously melted with the bain-marie method, and working in the sugar a pinch of salt, the grated rind of the lemon, the rest of the flour, 2 egg yolks and 1 stiffly beaten egg white.
Knead for a considerable time, adding a little more milk or a little water if the dough is too solid; leave to rise in a warm, dark place.
In the meantime, prepare the filling: grind finely the walnuts, the almonds and the pine kernels; mince the raisins, first washed and soaked in a little Grappa; scald the cinnamon in a pan with a little butter.
In a bowl, mix these ingredients with the cocoa, the sugar, the rum, the Grappa and a pinch of grated nutmeg. Knead the dough again, adding the 2 yolks that remain and the small glass of rum; work the dough thoroughly to a smooth consistency.
Place the dough on a floured cloth and roll it out with a rolling pin to a

thickness of a few millimetres. Spread the filling on the pastry and a few knobs of butter; with the aid of the cloth, roll up the stuffed pastry and place it on an oven tray (possibly lined with oven paper), making it into the characteristic snail shape of the *gubana*.

Cover with a cloth and leave it to rise for a time in a warm place.

When it has risen, brush the surface of the dessert with a beaten egg yolk and cook it in a pre-heated oven (180°C) for about 40 minutes. Before serving, dust with sugar.

CREAM MERINGUES

◆

150 g of sugar, 3 egg whites, ½ l of single cream, flour, butter, icing sugar.

Whip the egg whites stiffly, grind the sugar in an electric food mixer to make it finer and more easily amalgamated, then sprinkle it on the whipped egg whites and fold it in delicately, being careful not to make the egg whites collapse. Pour the mixture into an icing bag and squirt it onto a buttered and lightly floured baking tray, making little heaps the shape of half eggs, or of little tufts.

Dust the meringues with a little icing sugar, then put into a moderate oven for about half an hour: the meringues must only become dry without cooking or darkening.

Before removing from the oven, check the cooking by removing one and breaking it open.

After cooling them, scrape out a little of each meringue from the flat bottom, fill with whipped cream and close it with another meringue, base to base.

Garnish with a little more cream, and possibly with a little plain cocoa powder.

139

MONTBLANC CAKE
◀ *The Aosta Valley* ▶ 🔳

600 g of chestnuts, 1 egg, 2 dl of single cream, 50 g of sugar, 20 g of butter, icing sugar, milk, 1 stick of vanilla.

Make a cut in the peel of the chestnuts and boil them, a few at a time, for about 10 minutes, in order to peel them easily (removing also the inner film). Place them on the heat in a casserole with the sugar and the vanilla, cover them again with the milk, cook on a very low heat (using a metal wire net to protect from the flames) for about 40 minutes, or, anyway, enough time as is necessary to absorb all the milk. Remove the vanilla and pass the chestnuts through a sieve; amalgamate them with a little milk in order to obtain a consistent cream; bind this with an egg yolk and the softened butter, and mix them together with a wooden spoon. Using a potato masher, press the chestnut mixture down on a serving plate, giving it the shape of a mountain. Whip the cream, sweetening it with a little icing sugar, and decorate the top of the mountain with this, making it look snowy. Chill in the refrigerator before serving.

CHOCOLATE MOUSSE

7 eggs, 350 g of plain chocolate, 125 g of sugar, 50 g of butter.

Mix thoroughly the sugar with the egg yolks, until they are well creamed. Dissolve the chocolate with the bainmarie method, after cutting it into small pieces, then remove from the heat and add the softened butter and the egg and sugar mixture. Whip stiffly the egg whites, and stir them in very delicately, taking care not to make them collapse, pour the mousse into single bowls and chill in the refridgerator for at least a couple of hours before serving.

NEPITELLE
◀ *Calabria* ▶

350 g of flour, 3 eggs, 100 g of ricotta cheese, 100 g of raisins, 50 g of lard, 30 g of sugar, 30 g of icing sugar, ½ lemon, ½ orange, 1 spoonful of brandy, salt.

Break up the ricotta in a bowl with a fork, then (preferably with a wooden spoon) mix in a spoonful of sugar. When it becomes creamy, add the minced raisins, the grated rind of the lemon and the orange and the brandy; mix all the ingredients thoroughly.
Form a mound of the flour on the table and in a well in the centre beat 2 eggs with a fork, adding the remaining sugar. Knead it with the fingers, gradually working together the eggs and the flour, then continue to knead it for about half an hour. Roll out the dough with a rolling pin, making two sheets of thin pastry; spread them with a beaten egg and a spoonful of water. On one of the sheets lay little heaps of the filling 3 cm from each other; lay the other sheet on top and press around the heaps of filling, to join the two sheets together. With a wheeled pasta cutter, cut out lots of little squares, arrange them on a baking tray greased with lard.
Cook in a pre-heated oven for about 40 minutes at moderate heat (200°C). Remove the *nepitelle* from the oven

when they are golden brown and dust with icing sugar.

COCONUT BALLS

◆

200 g of grated coconut pulp, 250 g of butter, 150 of icing sugar, 1 spoonful of plain cocoa, 1 spoonful of rum.

Work the butter well (having previously softened it at room temperature) until it becomes a soft cream, add the sugar and continue to mix, keeping the mixture soft and creamy. Always stirring, add the cocoa dissolved in the rum and three quarters of the grated coconut. When everything is thoroughly mixed, remove the dough, one spoonful at a time, and with the fingers form little balls, and cover them with the remaining grated coconut. Chill in the fridge for a few hours before serving.

PANDORO

◀ *Veneto* ▶

500 g of flour, 200 g of sugar, 200 g of butter, 40 g of yeast, 5 eggs, vanillin.

The recipe for the famous Veronese *pandoro* is well protected by the industries that produce the mythical cake. We offer this which, although with no pretensions, will help you to produce a home-made *pandoro* not at all to be despised.

In a large bowl knead the yeast, 90 g of flour, an egg yolk and 10 g of sugar; cover with a clean cloth and leave to stand in a warm place for 3-4 hours. Then knead 150 g of flour with 30 g of butter melted with the bain-marie method, 70 g of sugar and 2 egg yolks.

Add this to the mixture prepared previously and, after having perfectly amalgamated them with long manual kneading, leave the dough to stand for another couple of hours. Then put the rest of the flour, 50 g of sugar, 30 g of melted butter, and 2 whole eggs into the dough, knead energetically, then leave to stand for another 2 hours.

After this time, knead a little more, adding a pinch of vanillin, then roll it out and place the rest of the butter in the middle.

Close the dough folding the corners in to form a packet then roll out roughly; repeat this operation twice more. Leave to stand for another half hour, then repeat the whole procedure again.

Finally, make a ball with the dough and put it into a deep buttered cake tin dusted with sugar and leave it to rise in a warm place. When the dough has reached the edge of the tin, cook it in a moderate oven for three quarters of an hour, lowering the heat after the first quarter of an hour.

PANETTONE
◀ Lombardy ▶

700 g of flour, 250 g of sugar, 225 g of butter, 200 g of raisins, 70 g of candied lime and orange peel, 6 eggs, 2 lemons, 20 g of yeast, 10 g of salt, almonds to decorate.

To prepare the rising dough, dissolve the yeast in a few spoonfuls of warm water, add 100 g of flour and enough water to obtain a consistent loaf of dough. Make an incision on the top in the shape of a cross and leave it to rise for about half an hour in a well covered receptacle in a warm place.
Put the rest of the flour in a large mixing bowl and knead it with the dough which was left to rise, adding enough water to reach the same consistency as before; leave it all to rise in a well floured bowl, well covered in a warm place until it has doubled in size. Then put the dough in a large mixing bowl again, and knead in the remaining flour, the butter, melted with the bain-marie method, the sugar dissolved with the egg yolks, a pinch of salt and the grat-

ed rind of the lemon; if necessary, add a little warm water to obtain a soft shiny dough.
Mix well the candied peel cut into tiny cubes and the raisins softened in warm water and dried and floured, then add them to the dough. Line a special cake tin (or, anyway, a deep, round tin) with paper greased with oil and butter, make an incision in the top in the shape of a cross and decorate with a few peeled almonds, pressing them lightly into the dough a little. Bake at 200°C for about 10 minutes, then lower the heat to 170°C and continue cooking for another 30 or 40 minutes.

COOKED CREAM
◀ The Aosta Valley, Piedmont ▶

500 g of cream, 200 g of icing sugar, 100 g of sugar, 50 g of milk, 2 1/2 sheets of fish glue, 1/2 stick of vanilla.

Heat the cream with the icing sugar (which can be produced just by grinding ordinary sugar in an electric food mixer); mix it until the sugar has completely dissolved, taking care not to bring to the boil. Remove from the heat.
Dissolve the fish glue in 2 spoonfuls of milk, then add them to the cream. Pour the sugar into individual bowls (or in a mould, if you wish to produce one single form) and caramelise it, then pour it over the cream. Leave it to cool down the refrigerator for a few hours and turn out to serve, or serve in the

individual bowls. If desired the caramel can be omitted; in this case, serve the cream together with raspberry syrup.

PANPEPATO
◀ *Umbria* ▶

350 g of flour, 250 g of honey, 125 g of almonds, 125 g of sugar, 2 eggs, 1 small lemon, 6 dl of oil, ¹/₂ envelope of baking powder for cakes, pimento, 1 clove, salt, pepper.

Melt the honey with the sugar and the oil in a casserole, stirring carefully. Mix the flour with the baking powder and a pinch of pepper, the pulverised clove, 2 pinches of pimento (a hot spice, similar to pepper, also called Jamaican pepper) and a pinch of salt. Mix together all the ingredients, adding the eggs one at a time, then add the honey syrup and the grated rind of the lemon.
Leave the dough to stand, covered with a cloth in a dark, cool place, then

make it into the desired shape and put it into the oven to cook.
Peppered bread is suitable for the preparation of little tarts or it can be covered with sugar icing or chocolate icing.

NEAPOLITAN *PASTIERA*
◀ *Campania* ▶

For the pastry: 200 g of wheat flour, 100 g of sugar, 100 g of butter, 2 eggs, salt.
For the filling: 500 g of ricotta cheese, 200 g of sugar, 200 g of precooked wheat or wheat softened for a few days in water, 50 g of icing sugar, 40 g of candied lime, 40 g of candied orange, 30 g of butter, 5 eggs, 2 dl of milk, 1 lemon, cinnamon, salt.

To prepare the pastry, making a mound of the flour mixed with the sugar on the work surface; in a well in the centre put the butter, softened and cut into small pieces, a whole egg, one egg yolk and a pinch of salt. Knead quickly until the dough is soft and even, then leave it to stand covered with a cloth for half an hour in a cool place.
Cook the wheat with the milk, the grated rind of half the lemon and the butter in a casserole, stirring continuously, for about ten minutes. Add the ricotta, the sugar, the grated rind of the remaining half lemon, a pinch of cinnamon and one of salt; knead it for some length until it is creamy, then add the roughly minced candied fruit. At this point add the yolks of 4 eggs, the wheat cream and lastly 3 stiffly whipped egg whites. Roll out

two thirds of the pastry dough to a thickness of about half a centimetre and line a greased and floured cake tin; pour the mixture onto the pastry lining, fold the edges towards the centre and, with the remaining pastry, form strips about half a centimetre thick and arrange them on top of the cake like a grating and brush them with the last remaining beaten egg.

Cook in a moderate oven for about an hour, and serve dusted with icing sugar.

RICCIARELLI
◀ Tuscany ▶

250 g of icing sugar, 150 g of sweet, shelled almonds, 15 bitter almonds, 1 egg, 20 wafers.

Remove the film from the almonds tossing them into boiling water, then put them into a hot oven for a few moments to dry them. When they are cold, reduce them to a powder with a pestle or with a food mixer, then mix with the icing sugar (keeping a little aside).Whip the egg whites stiffly, then delicately fold in the almond paste, one spoonful at a time. When the mixture becomes too stiff to work with a spoon, knead it manually on the work surface dusted with icing sugar. When the mixture is even, roll it out with a rolling pin to a thickness of about 1 cm and a half and cut out discs as big as the wafers. Place the wafers on a baking tray and put a disc of almond paste on each wafer, cover with a cloth and leave to stand for about an hour in a cool place. Cook in a moderately hot oven (without browning them)for about half an hour, remove from the oven, cool and serve, after cutting off any protruding parts of wafer and dusting with icing sugar.

CANDIED PEEL
◀ Sicily ▶

1 kg of citrus fruits, 750 g of sugar.

Untreated oranges, lemons, grapefruit and, if possible, limes are necessary; wash them carefully, dry them and cut them into segments about 1 cm wide leaving some of the pulp attached to the peel; boil them separately in water for about 15 minutes and, always keeping them separate, put them into a large frying pan together with two thirds of their weight of sugar: for a kilo of fruit about 750 g of sugar are needed.

Caramelise the fruit on a high heat, taking care not to burn the sugar; remove the peel from the heat when the sugar has reached a good consistency and a golden colour; leave it to cool on a marble surface and roll them in a layer of sugar. Keep them in an airtight jar.

SBRISOLONA

◀ *Lombardy* ▶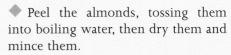

200 g of wheat flour, 200 g of finely ground corn flour, 200 g of almonds, 150 of sugar, 120 g of butter, 100 g of lard, 2 eggs, 1 lemon, icing sugar, vanillin, salt.

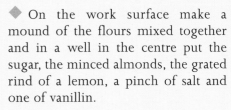

◆ Peel the almonds, tossing them into boiling water, then dry them and mince them.

◆ On the work surface make a mound of the flours mixed together and in a well in the centre put the sugar, the minced almonds, the grated rind of a lemon, a pinch of salt and one of vanillin.

◆ Mix the ingredients together thoroughly, then form the mound again and in the centre place the softened butter and the lard and knead again. It is impossible to obtain a smooth dough, but it is important that the ingredients are well amalgamated.

◆ Put the dough into a greased and floured cake tin, crumbling it up and forming an even layer; before putting into the oven, knock it on the work surface a few time to remove any possible empty spaces there could have formed. Cook in a hot oven for about one hour, leave to cool and serve dusted with icing sugar.

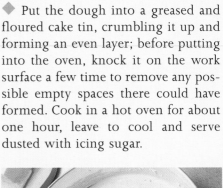

HONEY *SEBADAS*
◀ *Sardinia* ▶

600 g of flour, 400 g of fresh Sardinian sheep's milk cheese, 6 eggs, bitter honey, 80 g of lard, oil for frying.

Make the flour into a mound on a pastry board, and place the eggs and the lard in the centre. Knead together to obtain a smooth dough. Roll out the dough into very thin pastry, and cut out little squares; in the centre of the squares put small pieces of fresh sheep's milk cheese; fold the squares in half, pressing on the edges to close them. Fry the *sebadas* in a frying pan with abundant oil and, once cooked, leave them on absorbent kitchen paper to drain; serve hot, drenched with a little liquefied bitter honey.

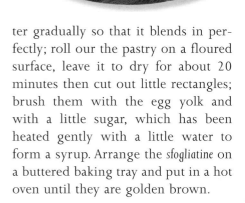

148

SFOGLIATINE
◀ *Veneto* ▶

350 g of flour, 200 g of butter, $\frac{1}{2}$ l of milk, 20 g of yeast, 4-5 spoonfuls of sugar, 1 egg, salt.

Work the flour with the sugar, milk, yeast and a pinch of salt. Add the butter gradually so that it blends in perfectly; roll our the pastry on a floured surface, leave it to dry for about 20 minutes then cut out little rectangles; brush them with the egg yolk and with a little sugar, which has been heated gently with a little water to form a syrup. Arrange the *sfogliatine* on a buttered baking tray and put in a hot oven until they are golden brown.

APPLE STRUDEL
◀ *Trentino Alto-Adige* ▶ 📷

<u>For the dough</u>: 250 g of flour, 1 egg, 2 spoonfuls of oil, salt.
<u>For the filling</u>: 2 kg of apples, 150 g of breadcrumbs, 250 g of sugar, 80 g of butter, 50 g of raisins, 50 g of pine kernels, cinnamon, lemon.

Arrange the flour on the work surface and with one hand knead it together with the eggs, the oil and a pinch of salt, while with the other hand pour water very gradually onto the flour until there is enough to

form the correct consistency. Knead the dough until it is smooth and elastic, then make a ball, lightly oil the ball, and leave it to stand in a cool, dark place.

In the meantime peel the apples, remove the cores, and cut them into thin slices, and toast the breadcrumbs in 150 g of butter. Roll out the dough on a floured cloth, using both a rolling pin and the hands; roll it out very thinly, taking care that it does not break, however. Brush the pastry with the remaining melted butter. Spread the filling on the pastry, leaving a strip at the end empty: first sprinkle with breadcrumbs, then a layer of apple slices, then sprinkle sugar on top, and then add the raisins, previously soaked in warm water and then squeezed to eliminate the excess liquid, and the pine kernels previously toasted in a frying pan, and the grated lemon peel. Very delicately, using the cloth under the pastry, roll up the strudel beginning with the end covered in the filling, place it on a greased baking tray and brush it with melted butter. Cook in a hot oven for about half an hour and serve the strudel still warm, dusting the surface with icing sugar.

TIRAMISÙ
◆

Pieces of sponge cake or sponge finger biscuits, Mascarpone cream, 3 cups of strong coffee, plain cocoa.

Cut the sponge cake into slices 1½ cm thick. Pour the coffee into a bowl and dip the sponge slices in the coffee (without completely drenching them) and then arrange them in a layer on a serving plate. Cover with the Marscarpone cream prepared in advance, cover with another layer of sponge slices dipped into the coffee. Finish with a layer of Mascarpone cream, then place the dessert in a refrigerator to chill; before serving dust the surface with an even layer of plain cocoa. Sponge finger biscuits can be used instead of the sponge cake.

TORCOLO
◀ *Umbria* ▶

400 g of flour, 200 g of sugar, 150 g of pine kernels, 50 g of candied fruit, 50 g of raisins, 1 egg, 10 g of bicarbonate of soda, 1 pinch of aniseeds, 60 g of butter, salt.

Cut the fruit into small cubes, mince the raisins, toast the pine kernels in the oven for about 3 minutes and pound them with a pestle and mortar. Make a mound of the flour on the table and in a well in the centre place the softened butter, the pine kernels, the sugar, the bicarbonate, the

aniseeds, the egg and a pinch of salt. Mix all the ingredients together, kneading them for a few minutes, add the candied fruit and the raisins and make it into a large doughnut. Place the torcolo on a buttered and floured baking tray, and cook in a moderate oven (200°C) for about half an hour, until the surface is golden brown. Leave it to cool before serving.

YOGHURT CAKE
◆

1 tube weighing 125 g of natural yoghurt, 1 tub of sugar, 3 tubs of flour, ½ tub of extra virgin olive oil, 3 eggs, 1 lemon, salt.

The most common version of this simple cake uses the same tub that contained the yoghurt for measuring the other ingredients. Mix carefully the egg yolks with the sugar, add the flour, the oil, the yoghurt, and the stiffly beaten egg whites. Add a pinch of salt and the grated lemon rind. Pour the mixture into a buttered and floured cake tin and cook for about three quarters of an hour in a pre-heated oven. When removed from the oven, the cake can be sprinkled with

150

icing sugar. Generally natural yoghurt is used, but the same excellent results are obtained also using banana yoghurt or apricot yoghurt.

CARROT CAKE
◀ *Trentino-Alto Adige* ▶

300 g of carrots, 300 g of shelled almonds, 300 g of sugar, 4 eggs, 1 lemon, 1 small glass of rum, 1 spoonful of flour.

Mix together well the sugar and the egg yolks until the mixture is smooth and creamy, then add, stirring carefully, the flour, the grated carrots, the minced almonds, the grated lemon rind and the liquor.
Last, fold in carefully the egg whites stiffly beaten. Pour the mixture into a greased and floured cake tin and cook in a hot oven for about three quarters of an hour. If you prefer, the cake can be made without the liquor and with a pinch of grated nutmeg and a little honey or lemon juice, instead.

BLACK MYRTLE BERRY CAKE
◀ *Trentino-Alto Adige* ▶

250 g of fine corn flour, 100 g of white flour, 300 g of black myrtle berries, 220 g of butter, 200 g of sugar, 20 g of honey, 1 sachet of vanillin, 1 sachet of yeast.

Mix the egg yolks with the sugar until the mixture is soft and creamy, then sprinkle on the corn flour, the wheat flour, the yeast and the vanillin. Soften the butter with the bain-marie method and add to the mixture, then add the stiffly beaten egg whites.

Grease and flour a round cake tin, pour in the mixture and put into a moderate oven for about one hour. When the cooking is finished, remove from the oven, and leave the cake to stand for about ten minutes, then cut it in half horizontally. In the meantime, wash and toss into boiling water for a few moments the myrtle berries. Mix them with a little honey and put this mixture between the two halves of the cake. Put the one half back on top of the other and serve.

RICOTTA CAKE
◀ *Campania* ▶

300 g of flour, 200 g of ricotta cheese, 100 g of pine kernels, 2 spoonfuls of honey, 80 g of butter, 1 spoonful of extra virgin olive oil, salt.

Prepare a dough with the flour, the butter, 1 spoonful of honey, a pinch of salt and a little water, and leave it to stand in the refrigerator for about half an hour. In the meantime, prepare the filling: put the ricotta into a bowl with the raisins, washed and softened in warm water, 50 g of the pine kernels, $\frac{1}{2}$ spoonful of honey, and a little grated vanilla.
Add about one glass of water and beat the mixture with an electric food mixer in order to obtain a thick cream. Put the remaining pine kernels, the egg, the remaining $\frac{1}{2}$ spoonful of honey, the oil and the grated lemon juice in a dish. Mix this with the ricotta mixture already prepared. Pour it onto a deep sided oiled and floured baking tray, and cook in a moderate oven for about an hour. Serve cold.

TAGLIATELLE CAKE
◀ Emilia Romagna ▶

For the pastry: 300 g of flour, 120 g of sugar, 80 g of butter, 2 eggs.
For the tagliatelle: wheat flour, 1 egg.
For the filling: 100 g of sugar, 100 g of butter, 120 g of sweet, shelled almonds, 15 g of shelled bitter almonds, 50 g of chocolate powder, 1 glass of Sassolino, the juice of ½ lemon.
To complete: 20 g of butter, 20 g of candied lime, icing sugar.

Make the pastry using the ingredients suggested. Mix the flour with the sugar and make a mound on the work surface. In the centre put the softened butter, cut into small pieces, the egg yolks, then knead quickly until the dough is soft and even; make it into a ball and leave it to stand for about half an hour, covered by a cloth.

To prepare the tagliatelle: use the egg and as much flour as is necessary to obtain a solid dough: knead it at length, then roll it out very thinly and leave it to dry for a little. Then roll it up and cut it into very thin tagliatelle, unroll them immediately on the floured work surface.

To prepare the filling, toss the sweet almonds in boiling water for a moment, peel them and toast them lightly in the oven. Then mince them and mix them with the butter, the sugar, the minced bitter almonds, the chocolate, the Sassolino and the lemon juice.

When the pastry dough has stood for the required length of time, roll it out with a rolling pin on the floured work surface; then line a cake tin with the pastry, put the filling into it and level it off. Cover the surface with the tagliatelle, pour the melted butter over it, cover with greased paper and cook in the oven at a moderate heat (180°C). After about half an hour, remove the cake from the oven, take off the greased paper, and sprinkle the surface with candied lime cut into very small pieces and dusted with the icing sugar. Leave the cake to stand in a cool place for a whole day before serving.

ZALETTI
◀ Veneto ▶

250 g of corn flour, 100 g of white corn flour, 30 g of raisins, 250 g of sugar, 6 eggs, 1 l of milk, 100 g of butter, 2 lemons, 1 stick of vanilla, salt.
For the cream: 4 egg yolks, 80 g of sugar, 2 spoonfuls of flour, ½ l of milk, 1 lemon.

Add a pinch of salt and the vanilla to the milk and bring it to the boil; remove the vanilla and sprinkle into it the milk the two kinds of corn flour, mixed and sifted. Mix together carefully, remove from the heat, and add the sugar and the butter; when it is well mixed leave to stand for a couple of hours.

In the meantime prepare the custard cream: mix the egg yolks and the sugar together in a deep casserole.
Then add the flour, little by little, with the sugar, add the boiling milk and the grated lemon rind. Put the casserole on the heat and bring to the boil stirring continuously; remove from the heat after boiling for 3 minutes and leave to cool. Fold the eggs into the flour mixture one at a time, then the grated rind of the lemons, the cooled custard cream, and the raisins softened in a little warm water and then drained and floured.
Put the mixture on a buttered baking tray, making small thickish disks about 5 cm in diameter. Cook them in a hot oven for about half an hour. Serve them warm and dusted with icing sugar.

ZELTEN

◀ Trentino Alto-Adige ▶

200 g of flour, 100 g of dried figs, 100 g of shelled walnuts and hazel nuts, 50 g of raisins, 50 g of pine kernels, 50 g of candied orange peel, 60 g of butter, 20 g of yeast, 1 egg, 2 cups of milk, 2 spoonfuls of honey, vanilla, shelled hazelnuts and almonds for decoration, salt.

Soften the raisins and the figs cut into small pieces in warm water. Mix the flour with a pinch of salt and make it into a mound in a large mixing bowl. Place the yeast dissolved in a little warm water and a spoonful of honey in a well in the centre. Mix the yeast with the flour and leave to rise for about half an hour. Then add the softened butter cut into small pieces, the remaining honey and the egg to the flour. Knead, adding a little milk in order to obtain a soft and creamy dough. At this point mix in the raisins and the figs, drained and squeezed, the pine kernels, the ground hazelnuts and walnuts, and the roughly ground candied orange peel.

When all the ingredients are well mixed, cover and leave to stand for a couple of hours in a warm place sheltered from draughts. Then place the dough in a greased and floured round cake tin, decorating the surface with a few almonds (which have tossed into boiling water, dried, and peeled) and walnuts, then cook in a hot oven for about an hour. *Zelten* should not be served immediately, but should be left for at least 36 hours after the cooking. If it is kept in a cool place, it can be conserved a long time.

St. Joseph's *Zeppole*
◀ *Campania* ▶

500 g of flour, 15 g of yeast, 100 g of sugar, 1 egg, 1 lemon, milk, 50 g of butter, olive oil, icing sugar.

Dissolve the yeast in a little warm water, breaking it up and pounding it, then add it to a little flour, mix well and make a soft dough; leave this to stand for half an hour. Then add the egg, a little warm milk, the sugar, the butter melted with the bain-marie method, the grated rind of the lemon and the rest of the flour. Knead the dough well until it is smooth and compact, then divide it up into small quantities and form little doughnuts. Leave them to rise on a floured cloth, then fry them in hot oil. Drain the *zep-*

pole when they are golden brown, and dry on absorbent kitchen paper, then drift with icing sugar.

Trifle
◆

Sponge cake or sponge finger biscuits, custard cream, 150 g of plain chocolate, alchèrmes, rum.

Cut the sponge cake into slices about 1 cm thick; then divide the cream (still hot) into two parts: add to one half the grated chocolate melted with the bain-marie method together with a couple of spoonfuls of water.

Prepare two plates: one for the alchèrmes, the other for the rum, to both of which has been added a little water. Butter a soup bowl and dust it with sugar, then place in it a layer of sponge cake soaked in the alchèrmes, and cover with a layer of chocolate flavoured custard cream; then place a layer of sponge cake soaked in rum on top, followed by a layer of ordinary custard cream.

Continue in this way, alternating the layers with the various ingredients, until they are all used up, finishing with a layer of cream evenly spread over the top. Leave the dessert for a few hours in the refrigerator to chill before serving; it can be decorated with little blobs of whipped cream, if desired. Instead of sponge cake, sponge finger biscuits can be used.

INDEX

Hors d'oeuvres

Ascolian olives	18
Aubergine hors d'oeuvre	9
Bagna caûda	10
Bruschetta (Olive oil toast)	12
Calf's head in salad	18
Cazzilli	12
Chicken liver croutons	13
Croutons *alla Ciociara*	14
Easter cake	20
Erbazzone (Tasty spinach pie)	14
Fettunta (Oiled slices)	14
Fried olives	19
Garnished olives	18
Italian hors d'oeuvre	8
Lemon crabs	15
Marinated anchovies	8
Mozzarella *in carrozza*	16
Mozzarella titbits	20
Mushroom vol-au-vents	24
Panzerotti (Tomato "tummies")	19
Parmesan and truffle	9
Pilchards in *saór*	20
Russian salad	16
Sage biscuits	11
Sage in batter	19
Scallops au gratin	12
Sea food salad	15
Shrimp boats	10
Shrimp cocktail	18
Shrimp vol-au-vents	23
Squid salad	23
Stuffed mussels	13
Sweet pepper roulades	16
Truffle croutons	13

Leavened breads, flat breads, pizzas, savoury cakes

Apulian bread	30
Carasau bread or *Carta musica*	29
Farinata (Chick pea bread)	28
Flat cheesy bread	28
Flat olive oil bread	28
Neapolitan pizza	32
Onion quiche	33
Pizza *Margherita* (Margaret's pizza)	32
Romagna *piadina*	30
Sea fruit pizza	31
Semolina cake	35
Sfinciuni	33
Spinach strudel	34
Tarallucci biscuits	35
Tuscan bread	30
Walnut bread	29

Sauces and dressings

Garlic dressing	38
Genoese *pesto*	38
Green sauce	38
Peará sauce	39

First courses

Agnolotti with truffles	42
Amatriciana bucatini	45
Baked *cannelloni*	46
Baked *lasagne*	50
Barley soup	53
Black cuttlefish spaghetti	69
Bolete mushroom risotto	66
Broad bean and chicory soup	82
Bucatini with lamb sauce	45
Canederli (Bacon balls)	46
Cappelletti (Pasta in broth)	46
Celery soup	84
Chestnut and milk soup	52
Chick pea soup	82
Cooked bread	55
Cooked water	42
Fettuccine alla romana (Roman style noodles)	48
Fish broth	44
Fusilli pasta with broad beans	49
Gnocchi alla valdostana (Aosta Valley dumplings)	49
Hazelnut *Pansotti*	55
Jota	50
Macaroni hash	59
Macaroni with ricotta cheese and sausage	51
Maize soup	84
Malloreddus	52
Mille cosedde	52
Mushroom *tagliatelle*	75
Neapolitan *Agnolotti*	42

MAIN MEAT COURSES